# OPPORTUNITIES

in

# Transportation
# Careers

# OPPORTUNITIES

## in

# Transportation Careers

### REVISED EDITION

**ADRIAN PARADIS**

New York   Chicago   San Francisco   Lisbon   London   Madrid   Mexico City
Milan   New Delhi   San Juan   Seoul   Singapore   Sydney   Toronto

**Library of Congress Cataloging-in-Publication Data**

Paradis, Adrian A.
    Opportunities in transportation careers / by Adrian Paradis. — 2nd ed., rev.
       p.   cm.
    ISBN 0-07-148209-1 (alk. paper)
    1. Transportation—Vocational guidance—United States.   I. Title.

    HE203.P28    2007
    388.023'73—dc22                       2007010423

1 2 3 4 5 6 7 8 9 10 11 12 13 14 15 16 17 18 19   DOC/DOC   0 9 8 7

ISBN 978-0-07-148209-7
MHID     0-07-148209-1

Interior design by Rattray Design

McGraw-Hill books are available at special quantity discounts to use as premiums and sales promotions, or for use in corporate training programs. For more information, please write to the Director of Special Sales, Professional Publishing, McGraw-Hill, Two Penn Plaza, New York, NY 10121-2298. Or contact your local bookstore.

This book is printed on acid-free paper.

# CONTENTS

management. Finding your job. Earnings.
Employment outlook.

# 1

# Lure of the Water

Shipping has been important to our economic and social growth for centuries. Small boats could carry passengers and freight along the coastlines of oceans, seas, lakes, and rivers more easily than traveling over land, which required cutting roads through forests and across deserts, often a difficult and dangerous undertaking, especially if hostile inhabitants were encountered. This preference for water transportation explains why civilization developed mostly along seacoasts and inland rivers.

## Our Oceangoing Heritage

At first this was true on the North American continent, too. Early explorers sailed along the New England coastline and farther south, some of them establishing tentative colonies on the edge of the forbidding forests. Were it not for those tiny ships manned by curious and courageous mariners who reached these shores, this vast continent might never have been discovered and settled.

Our oceangoing heritage traces back to those voyagers who reached these shores, who sailed here from Europe and subsequently traded along the Atlantic seaboard and down to the West Indies. Many early settlers became shipbuilders, thanks to the unlimited source of lumber and good prospects of trans-Atlantic trade with mother countries where markets for New World products were growing.

Although American privateers were active during the Revolutionary War, it was the French fleet that contributed to the final British surrender at Yorktown. Realizing the need to build a strong navy, the new American Congress authorized construction of the USS *Constitution* ("Old Ironsides"), a forty-four-gun frigate that took part in the Tripolitan War and the War of 1812 and today is enshrined in Boston Harbor.

America has a proud heritage of ocean transportation. Following the War of 1812, the swift packet boats and merchant ships carried most of the coastal and trans-Atlantic passenger and freight traffic. Gradually steamships were introduced, followed by the outstanding marine development of the famous clipper ships, designed for speedy travel between the United States and China for the tea and opium trades.

With the discovery of gold in California, prospectors from the United States and Canada who wanted to avoid the dangerous overland trip from the East Coast chose to travel by ocean, either sailing around Cape Horn or shortening the trip by leaving the ships at the Isthmus of Panama, making their way across land to the Pacific, and completing the journey by water. As California continued to grow, it becaame the central location for all the rolling stock, rails, and equipment used to construct the western part of the transcontinental railroad. However, once the rails had met at Promontory Point, Utah, and trains started running from east to west, much of the former ocean freight and passenger business shifted to the rails.

Following the Civil War, England's new steel ships gave her a wide advantage over other nations, including the United States, which were slower to build similar merchant marine fleets (a nation's fleet of commercial ships). By the mid-1930s America's merchant marine had declined so far that Congress passed the Merchant Marine Act of 1936 to subsidize construction of a merchant marine and provide for appointment of a maritime commission to stimulate shipbuilding.

Soon the country greatly expanded its merchant marine to meet the demands of World War II, but that vast fleet proved unnecessary once the war had ended. Trans-Atlantic passenger traffic picked up again with the reappearance of luxurious liners, the best known of which flew the colors of England, France, Holland, Italy, and the United States. After the late 1950s, however, jet airlines cut trans-Atlantic travel times from four or five days to just hours, and by 1996 the only prestige ship still sailing from the United States was the *Queen Elizabeth II*, which offered special inducement fares for travelers who wanted to sail one way and jet back. For those who craved an ocean voyage, numerous cruise lines offered luxurious accommodations on various itineraries, and the cruise industry continues to grow today. Meanwhile, owners of many cargo ships had transferred their registries to countries such as Panama or Liberia, which assessed much lower taxes and had less stringent safety requirements.

## United States Merchant Marine

The United States Merchant Marine consists of a fleet of privately owned, U.S.-registered merchant ships that provide waterborne transportation for cargoes moving in domestic and international commerce.

The nation's economic and security needs met by the U.S. Merchant Marine are compelling. Today, the United States imports approximately 85 percent of some seventy-seven strategic commodities that are deemed critical to America's industry and defense. Although as a nation we account for only 6 percent of the world population, we purchase nearly a third of the world's output of raw materials. Ninety-nine percent of these materials are transported by merchant vessels.

## Merchant Marine Unlicensed Sailors

The Military Sealift Command (MSC), Department of the Navy, operates numerous merchant-type ships manned by civilian crews employed under civil service regulations. Previous U.S. Navy or U.S. Coast Guard experience is a major consideration in filling available jobs, which are based on wage rates and practices that are similar to the commercial shipping industry.

The National Oceanic Atmospheric Administration (NOAA), Office of Marine and Aviation Opportunities, operates high seas and inland oceanographic research and survey vessels. Most of the operating personnel are under civil service regulations.

### Job Descriptions

On a typical merchant ship, sailors make up most of the crew with each worker being assigned to one of the following departments: deck, engine, or steward. Check out these maritime job descriptions from the Military Sealift Command (MSC) to learn about the type of work you can perform in the maritime industry:

- **Ordinary seaman.** The ordinary seaman stands watch while in port or at sea and performs routine deck department maintenance tasks, such as cleaning, painting, and preserving the ship.
- **Able-bodied seaman.** In addition to performing the same duties as the ordinary seaman, the able-bodied seaman is also responsible for operating hydraulic equipment used during underway replenishment. This involves moving pallets loaded with supplies (such as food, clothing, and repair parts for machinery) to another ship while both ships are in motion. Underway replenishment is conducted either by using cables that connect the two ships or by helicopter between the two ships' flight decks.
- **Utility man (food handler).** The duties of the utility man include general hotel service work such as food handling, cleaning and maintaining staterooms and passageways, assisting the chief steward with daily provisions, and manning the hydraulic equipment used for the underway replenishment of supplies to other ships.
- **Engine utility man.** The engine utility man assists licensed engineers and performs general maintenance and repair of the ship's machinery; material handling equipment, including elevators and winches; and various other onboard machinery.
- **Deck engineer machinist.** The deck engineer machinist fabricates replacement parts utilizing various types of machinery.
- **Unlicensed junior engineer.** Unlicensed junior engineers stand engine-room watch, assist licensed engineers with control-room operations, and maintain the shipboard propulsion equipment and auxiliary machinery.
- **Second electrician.** The second electrician performs routine maintenance, repair, and operation of the ship's electrical systems.
- **Refrigeration engineer.** The refrigeration engineer maintains and repairs all types of onboard refrigeration and air-conditioning

equipment, including large cargo-hold systems, containers, small stateroom refrigerators, food service equipment, air-conditioning compressors, filtering systems, and all other refrigeration equipment.

• **Electronics technician.** The electronics technician is required to be proficient in the use of all electrical and electronic test and monitoring equipment during repairs and maintenance on electrical and electronic equipment aboard ship.

• **Wiper.** The wiper's duties include general engine department maintenance, cleaning, painting, preservation of the ship, and assisting unlicensed and licensed engineering department personnel with machinery repairs.

## *Working Conditions*

Working on a ship can subject you to great temperature extremes. Standing on the deck in the hot sun or during bitter cold, windy weather for long periods as a lookout can be as uncomfortable as working in the engine room with its constant high temperature.

Accommodations for sailors are not luxurious, but good meals are served in a mess room, which may double as a recreation hall. On older ships, crew members share quarters and have little privacy, but new vessels have single-berth rooms. However, even with improved conditions, work on a ship can become monotonous and tiresome.

Sailors in the merchant marine work seven days a week, usually serving on two four-hour watches or shifts during each twenty-four-hour period, and they have eight hours off between each watch. Some sailors are day workers, who are on duty eight hours a day from Monday through Friday. Overtime is paid for working beyond forty hours a week; when the ship is in port, the basic work-week is forty hours for all crew members.

## *Job Training*

Sailors and unlicensed engineers working on U.S. flagged deep-sea and Great Lakes vessels must hold a document issued by the Coast Guard. In addition, they must hold certification when working aboard liquid-carrying vessels. Able seamen are also required to carry government-issued certification.

To work as an unlicensed seaman, you will need a merchant mariner's document issued by the coast guard. Although you must be a U.S. citizen to fill most positions, a small percentage of applicants for merchant mariner documents do not need to be U.S. citizens; however, aliens must be legally admitted into the United States and hold a green card.

You will also need a medical certificate indicating excellent health and attesting to adequate vision, color perception, and general physical condition to work as a higher-level deckhand or unlicensed engineer. Although no experience or formal schooling is required, training at a union-operated school provides the best background. As a beginner, you will be classified as an ordinary seaman and may be assigned to any of the three unlicensed departments: deck, engine, or steward. With experience at sea and perhaps union-sponsored training, you can pass the able-seaman exam and move up with three years of service.

You do not need special training or experience to become a seaman or deckhand on vessels operating in harbors or on rivers or other waterways. Newly hired workers generally are given a short introductory course and then learn skills on the job. After sufficient experience, you will be eligible to take a coast guard exam to qualify as a mate, pilot, or captain, but you'll need substantial knowledge gained through experience, courses taught at approved schools, and independent study to pass the exam.

The Maritime Administration of the U.S. Department of Transportation (DOT) offers a wealth of information about education and training for a career as a merchant mariner. The DOT website lists maritime high schools, technical training schools, colleges, and academies throughout the country. For more information about these training opportunities, visit www.marad.dot.gov/acareera float/edtraining.htm.

## Merchant Marine Officers

So far we have described employment opportunities for seamen who make up the largest group of workers aboard a ship. Those in charge of the vessel are the ship's officers, headed by the captain, who has complete responsibility and authority for operating the ship as well as for the safety of the passengers, crew, cargo, and the vessel itself. Serving beneath the captain are officers in the deck and engine departments, as well as a purser, who is a staff officer. The purser handles all the required paperwork, including payrolls, and assists passengers as needed. Some pursers also have been trained as physician's assistants.

There are two ways to qualify for a deck or engineering officer's license. You either must accumulate sea time and meet regulatory requirements, or you must graduate from the U.S. Merchant Marine Academy or one of the six state maritime academies. In both cases, you will be required to pass a written examination. Federal regulations also require that you pass a physical examination, a drug screening, and a National Driver Register Check before being considered.

Without formal training, you can be licensed if you pass the written exam and possess sea service appropriate to the license for which you are applying. However, this option presents two obstacles: it is difficult to pass the examination without substantial formal schooling or independent study, and because seamen may work six or fewer months a year, it can take five to eight years to accumulate the necessary experience.

The state academies are the California Maritime Academy in Vallejo; Great Lakes Maritime Academy in Traverse City, Michigan; Maine Maritime Academy in Castine; Massachusetts Maritime Academy on Cape Cod; State University of New York Maritime College in Throgs Neck; and Texas Maritime Academy in Galveston. These schools offer a four-year academic program leading to a Bachelor of Science degree, a license (issued only by the coast guard) as a third mate (deck officer) or third assistant engineer (engineering officer), and, if you are qualified, a commission as ensign in the U.S. Naval Reserve, Merchant Marine Reserve, or Coast Guard Reserve. With experience and additional training, third officers may qualify for higher rank.

The following section will profile the Great Lakes Maritime Academy as an example of what you can expect at these specialized schools.

## Great Lakes Maritime Academy

Perhaps you are interested in a career as an officer aboard a ship that serves ports on the Great Lakes. The lake fleet and its personnel are part of the U.S. Merchant Marine, and there is a continuing need for highly trained men and women to operate these ships.

The Great Lakes Maritime Academy is a division of Northwestern Michigan College (NMC) and a partner of Ferris State University. The academy trains men and women to serve as business professionals and merchant marine officers aboard Great Lakes and ocean ships.

Great Lakes Maritime is designated as a regional maritime academy and the nation's only freshwater academy. Graduates are qualified to sail the Great Lakes or oceans and are awarded both a bachelor's degree in business administration and an associate's in maritime technology.

Successful cadets will be qualified to take the U.S. Coast Guard (USCG) examination for a third mate Great Lakes or oceans unlimited tonnage, first class pilot Great Lakes (deck program), or third assistant engineer, steam and motor vessels of any horsepower (engineering program). Cadets are part of the student body of NMC and may choose to live in resident halls with other students. They are not required to follow a rigid military schedule. They are, however, required to meet academic standards and demonstrate the self-discipline, leadership, and ship's officer qualities required in the exercise of good seamanship and engineering practices.

The Maritime Academy offers two career paths. Cadets who choose the "deck" program train to become pilots and mates, navigating ships through open waters and narrow harbors. Ships may stretch to one thousand feet in length and weigh several thousand tons. Graduates may also find satisfying careers in the tug/barge industry.

Cadets who choose the "engine" program train to become the power-plant engineers who operate the massive diesel or steam engines that drive these mighty vessels. Like a self-contained floating city, each freighter is supported by complex systems that require highly skilled attention.

Candidates for admission to Great Lakes must meet the following requirements:

- Be a citizen of the United States (Certain non-U.S. citizen candidates may be accepted for specialized programs not leading to licensing under USCG regulations. Potential candidates who have applied for U.S. citizenship and expect to complete the naturalization process prior to graduation may also apply.)
- Meet USCG requirements to qualify for an original license as a U.S. Merchant Marine Officer, including physical, vision, and moral character standards as are established by federal law and/or regulations
- Be seventeen years of age or older (no upper age limit)
- Possess a high school diploma or equivalent

Complete information about the academy, including all admission requirements, application procedures, and program descriptions, is available at www.nmc.edu/maritime.

## Portside Jobs

A ship at sea does not operate in a vacuum but depends on a framework of shore-side activities for its operations. The maritime industry includes companies that own and manage the vessels, ports and terminals where cargo is handled, yards for ship repair, marine insurance underwriters, ship-chartering firms, admiralty lawyers, engineering and research companies, and, increasingly today, intermodal systems of trucks and railroads to distribute goods around the country.

In the old days, stevedores, or longshoremen, performed all of the manual labor of carrying cargo on and off vessels, but much of that work is now performed by lift trucks and cranes, which cut down the need for manual workers. The introduction of containerization has also reduced the employment of longshoremen, but there are still opportunities for these workers, such as those described here.

Carloaders load and unload railroad cars, trucks, containers, and barges. Ship cleaners clean the ship's hold, wash painted surfaces, clean and check lifeboats and living quarters, and perform other duties. Marine carpenters crate and pack cargo, repair pallets, and do other work related to wood. Timekeepers keep track of work performed on the docks, ships, barges, and terminals. Billing and manifest clerks do the paperwork, while checkers keep track of all goods received or shipped. In addition there is the usual cadre of guards, mechanics, crane operators, ship maintenance personnel, truck drivers, and other workers.

Most ports have an organization called a *port authority*, which controls activities of the harbor. Many of them have training programs and may be helpful in giving advice about employment. You can find out about such programs by visiting the American Association of Port Authorities at www.aapa-ports.org.

Although many harbor workers learn on the job, clerical and technical skills can be learned in high school or a vocational school. A college degree or previous experience as a ship's officer is helpful when applying for the administrative jobs.

One other area in the portside is the familiar tugboat, which in some harbors is essential for pulling the larger ships into and out of the harbor as well as for towing barges. Here is an opportunity to work on a ship without ever going to sea.

## Inland Maritime Careers

You might not be familiar with the extensive inland waterway system that includes the Great Lakes, the Intracoastal system, rivers such as the "Mighty Mississippi," and Canada's Saint Lawrence Seaway. Actually about 15 percent of America's total transportation now moves on its inland waters, and the Saint Lawrence Seaway is one of the few great ship canals of the world, carrying freight to and from the heart of North America and the rest of the world.

Barges carry much of this freight, which consists principally of chemicals, grains, forest products, iron, steel, and petroleum products. These vessels are not manned nor are they self-propelled, but they are pulled by a tug or pushed by a towboat.

This is a different world from that of the merchant marine. Instead of three departments, each with its set of specialists, most towboats have a crew of two, the captain or master and the pilot or mate. They work together closely, each standing two six-hour watches per day. If it is a longer route there may be a second mate, and they stand two four-hour watches per day, the same as seamen. Those boats that ply the western rivers or the Gulf of Mexico inland waterways need a steersman, who steers the vessel while an engineer is on duty down in the hold of the engine room if it is a larger boat. Towboat cooks are responsible for serving the food they prepare, but deckhands may perform this work on smaller boats.

Responsibilities of the deckhand vary according to the size of the boat and its cargo. Aside from routine duties on the boat, the deckhand ties together the barges to be pulled and later breaks them apart when they reach their port of destination. He or she usually works six hours on, six off, a certain number of days on and off each month, creating a type of schedule and lifestyle that will not appeal to everyone. The work can be dangerous and boring, too, but the chance to travel over the waterways has a definite appeal to many.

Another important position is that of the tanker man, who loads and unloads liquid cargoes. En route, the tanker man watches the condition of the liquid and checks pumps and engines. He or she may also work in ports, refueling seagoing vessels from bunker barges.

## Other Marine Careers

You don't have to join the merchant marine to find a career in water transportation. Opportunities may lie close to your home if you live on or near the shore. Consider some of the following.

Operation of all-day fishing boats for those who enjoy the sport of deep-sea fishing is a growing business. Boats usually leave early in the morning and return sometime during the late afternoon. It is a common sight in an oceanfront resort community to see fishing boats lined up at the dock, each advertising its rates and schedules. You might find good summer or part-time employment that will give you valuable experience working as a hand on a fishing charter.

In some areas commercial fishing boats depart for distant fishing grounds and remain at sea for several days or weeks as they fill their holds with valuable catches. Even a short-term job on one of these boats can provide experience.

The growth and popularity of private boating has created an expanding marina business. A busy marina is an interesting place to work. Although you may not do much traveling, you'll learn how to handle boats and occasionally have a chance to get out on the water. In the north, marinas are a summer business and, therefore, offer only temporary jobs.

In many parts of the country, excursion boats take passengers to distant points of interest or just for a tour of the harbor. They provide jobs for deckhands, engineers, and others in the maritime field, as do ferries. Moonlight and dinner cruises are popular in many areas and may employ high school and college students as waiters or waitresses, reservation clerks, cleaners, and in various kitchen positions.

Look at the travel section of a Sunday newspaper and see how many ads there are for cruises. Cruise lines offer itineraries that range from three-day trips to around-the-world voyages. Crew members generally sign a contract to work for four or five months at a time; this is followed by one or two months off before their next sailing.

Many of today's cruise ships are of foreign registry, which means that they do not have to observe the stringent American rules that apply to the operation of passenger liners. However, ships that are owned and operated by foreign companies are usually staffed by natives of those countries. This may not be true of all the ships that call at a port near you and certainly not of excursion boats, which offer simple daytime or overnight trips. Since cruise ships are, in reality, floating hotels with every conceivable service for passengers, the list of job opportunities is long.

For more information about opportunities in the coast guard, see Chapter 9.

## Earnings

Earnings vary widely with the particular water transportation position and the worker's experience, ranging from the minimum wage for some beginning seamen or mate positions to more than $42 an hour for some experienced ship engineers. The most current available statistics from the U.S. Department of Labor show median hourly earnings in various occupations in 2004:

| | |
|---|---|
| Ship engineers | $26.42 |
| Captains, mates, and pilots of water vessels | $24.20 |
| Motorboat operators | $15.39 |
| Sailors and marine oilers | $14.00 |

Annual pay for captains of larger vessels, such as container ships, oil tankers, or passenger ships, may exceed $100,000, but only after many years of experience. Similarly, captains of tugboats often earn more than the median reported here, with earnings dependent on the port and the nature of the cargo.

Crew members of American merchant ships enjoy excellent pay as well as working and living conditions. Most jobs provide thirteen days or more of paid vacation for every thirty days worked. An example of typical pay on a modern merchant vessel in 2006 is shown in Table 1.1.

**Table 1.1 Typical Pay on Modern Merchant Vessels**

| | Officer Ratings | | |
|---|---|---|---|
| | *Monthly Base* | *Overtime* | *Total* |
| Third assistant engineer | $3,510 | $3,175 | $6,685 |
| Third mate | $3,510 | $3,175 | $6,685 |
| Radio officer | $4,938 | $4,466 | $9,404 |

| | Crew Ratings | | |
|---|---|---|---|
| | *Monthly Base* | *Overtime* | *Total* |
| Able seaman | $2,419 | $2,188 | $4,607 |
| Qmed (qualified member of the engine department) | $3,441 | $3,113 | $6,554 |
| Engine utility | $2,500 | $2,261 | $4,761 |
| Chief cook | $2,528 | $2,287 | $4,815 |
| Food handler | $1,680 | $1,519 | $3,199 |

## Employment Outlook

Employment in water transportation occupations is projected to increase only up to 8 percent through the year 2014, with most job growth occurring as a result of increasing tourism and increases in shipping traffic due to rising imports that will provide greater employment in and around major port cities.

After several years of decline, employment in deep-sea shipping for American mariners is expected to stabilize. International regulations have raised shipping standards with respect to safety, training, and working conditions, which means that competition from ships that sail under foreign flags of convenience has lessened as the standards of operation become more uniform. This has made the costs of operating a U.S. ship more comparable to foreign-flagged ships and has modestly increased the amount of international cargo carried by U.S. ships. Because a fleet of deep-sea U.S.-flagged ships is considered to be vital to the nation's defense, some receive federal support through a maritime security subsidy and other provisions in laws that limit certain federal cargoes to ships that fly the U.S. flag.

Employment growth also is expected in passenger cruise ships within U.S. waters. Vessels that operate between ports in the United States are required by law to be U.S.-flagged vessels. The planned building and staffing of several new cruise ships that will travel around the Hawaiian Islands should create new opportunities for employment at sea in the cruise line industry, which is composed mostly of foreign-flagged ships. Efforts are also under way at the federal level that could lead to greater use of ferries to handle commuter traffic around major metropolitan areas, and more workers may be hired.

Moderating the growth in water transportation occupations is a projected decline in vessels operating in the Great Lakes and inland waterways. Vessels on rivers and canals and on the Great Lakes carry mostly bulk products, such as coal, iron ore, petroleum, sand and gravel, grain, and chemicals. Although shipments of most of these products are expected to grow through the year 2014, imports of steel are dampening employment on the Great Lakes.

Job openings will also result from the need to replace those leaving the occupation. Some experienced merchant mariners may continue to go without work for varying periods. However, this situation appears to be changing, with demand for licensed and unlicensed personnel rising. Maritime academy graduates who have not found licensed shipboard jobs in the U.S. Merchant Marine may find jobs in related industries. Because they are commissioned as ensigns in the Naval or Coast Guard Reserve, some are selected for active duty in those branches of the service. Some find jobs as seamen on U.S.-flagged or foreign-flagged vessels, tugboats, and other watercraft or enter civilian jobs with the U.S. Navy or Coast Guard. Some take land-based jobs with shipping companies, marine insurance companies, manufacturers of boilers or related machinery, or other related jobs.

### Employment Statistics

Water transportation workers hold more than seventy-two thousand jobs in the United States. The total number who worked at some point in the year is perhaps twice as large because many merchant marine officers and seamen worked only part of the year. The following list shows employment in the occupations that make up this group:

| | |
|---|---|
| Captains, mates, and pilots of water vessels | 29,000 |
| Sailors and marine oilers | 28,000 |
| Ship engineers | 12,000 |
| Motorboat operators | 3,400 |

About 33 percent of all transportation workers are employed in water transportation services. About 17 percent work in inland water transportation, primarily the Mississippi River system, while the other 16 percent are employed in water transportation on the deep seas, along the coasts, and on the Great Lakes. Another 25 percent work in establishments related to port and harbor operations, marine cargo handling, or navigational services to shipping. The federal government employs approximately 5 percent of all water transportation workers, most of whom work on supply ships and are civilian mariners of the Navy's Military Sealift Command.

# 2

# From Trails to Superhighways

We have already seen how small boats transported goods and people before roads were constructed. With the invention of the wheel and the introduction of draft animals, it became possible to reach areas not previously accessible by water and thus open up vast new trading markets. Ancient civilizations constructed fine highways, and as early as 2700 B.C. China had a road system. Around 2000 B.C. Babylon and Ninevah built excellent roads and later a brick road was laid between the two cities. The Egyptian king who erected the Great Pyramid first spent ten years using one hundred thousand men to build a stone highway so materials could be moved to the pyramid site. However, the world had never seen such a road network as that which connected Rome with all parts of her empire.

The Romans built fifty thousand miles of roads to all major European cities so they could reach their conquered lands easily, move troops if necessary, and keep in touch with their armies. The roads were intended to protect the empire, not encourage trade, but because they were so well constructed, it was possible to transport goods quickly and economically. Nothing stopped the Roman road builders from using the most direct route. When they came to a river, they built a bridge. At a marsh, they filled the bog, and they tunneled through hills that stood in their way. Messengers on horseback could travel a hundred miles a day, and goods could be shipped from England to Rome in thirteen days, going to the coast of Gaul (France) and then by road to the Eternal City. After the fall of the Roman Empire, many roads were neglected, and it was not until the twentieth century that significant road building resumed.

## Earliest North American Roads

The first roads on the land that later became the United States and Canada were trails found on the midwest plains and in the forests along the Atlantic seaboard. Those out west were paths worn through tall grasses by buffalo and other animals as they chose the easiest routes to reach their feeding grounds, water holes, and nearby streams.

Along the Atlantic seaboard the Indians made their own trails through the forests. Most were eighteen or twenty inches wide and allowed the braves to remain hidden from enemies as they walked single file. This was ample width for a squaw who followed her brave, carrying all their possessions on her back.

These paths usually followed streams, with necessary crossings being made at shallow pools or across rocks. To ascend a hill, the Indian trails wound snakelike through the woods along the side of a slope, which made climbing easier. The early colonists used these trails for roads as they traveled by foot or on horseback from village to village. Gradually woodsmen widened the trails, and they then were referred to as roads.

Woodsmen marked trees at a road's start to indicate what type of road it was. One ax mark meant it was a one-chop road, wide enough for horseback riders. Once the road was broadened so two wagons could pass, two marks were blazed on the trees, and it was known as a two-chop road. When the ground became smooth enough for coaches, the three ax marks designated it as a three-chop road.

Some of the early short roads between New York and Boston, called *post roads*, were used by riders who carried mail from town to town. In 1673 mail was dispatched from New York to Boston for the first time. The road was so rutted, and at times muddy, that few wagons made the trip until 1772, when these primitive highways were considered safe enough for stagecoach travel (although still bumpy and, at times, almost impassable).

That same year a retired Virginia judge, Richard Henderson, eager to sell plots of land in Kentucky, organized the Transylvania Company to buy a large section of the wilderness. He asked his friend Daniel Boone to purchase the land from the Cherokee Indians who owned it. Once Boone accomplished this in the spring of 1775, he hired thirty men to help him carve out a roadway from North Carolina through the Cumberland Gap and into Kentucky. When the road builders reached the Kentucky River, they erected a fort, and within a short time, the new road was crowded with families hurrying west to buy land and build homes. Other roads followed, and soon those pioneers who were eager to leave the East could reach the fertile lands beyond the Alleghenies.

In the northeast, the Canada Road served as the primary link between lower Canada and Maine from 1820 to 1860. The road began as settlers from the Kennebec Valley in Maine moved north and the American pioneers found themselves closer to the markets of Quebec City than to those of Boston. Quebec was a growing lumber and shipbuilding port, as well as a military and administrative center. The city needed provisions, so American drovers took livestock north through the woods on a trail they built between the roads that lay alongside Maine's Kennebec and Canada's Chaudière Rivers, which served to close the gap between the two road systems.

In 1815 the road Chemin de la Chaudière, along the northeast shore of the Chaudière River, was extended to the fork of the DuLoup River in southeastern Quebec. It continued up the northeast shore of the DuLoup to just below the frontier. The twenty-eight-mile roadway was almost eighteen feet wide and followed the earlier drovers' trail.

## Turnpike Era

With the Revolutionary War behind them, many Americans living in the congested cities and suburbs along the Atlantic seaboard hoped to move west to buy land and establish new homes, farms, and businesses. However, it was a daunting trip, for there were few passable wagon roads and fewer inns or taverns to welcome the weary travelers.

The new federal government had no funds to plan, build, or repair roads, so many wealthy businessmen who needed to travel used their own money to help pay for better roads in their areas. They assisted in establishing companies that would build new highways and charge those who used them. These roads were laid out as straight as the land would permit and avoided steep grades or hills wherever possible. They were called turnpikes because each tollgate had a long pole studded with pikes (now called spikes) to close the highway until the traveler paid his toll. Once paid, the pole was swung back so the individual or wagon could pass through. Between 1792 and 1810 it has been estimated that there were 175 private companies in New England operating nearly three thousand miles of turnpikes.

The first important turnpike was built from Philadelphia to Lancaster, Pennsylvania, in 1791. Instead of the usual narrow, winding road, the Lancaster Turnpike Company constructed a highway twenty-four feet wide and paved it with a new type of surface invented by John L. McAdam, a Scottish engineer. It was made of crushed limestone and gravel called *macadam*. Horses and wagons passing over the road crushed the stone and packed it down even more firmly so that when it rained, the water ran off this surface into ditches on either side. For the first time travelers were free from delays caused by mud and ruts.

Other turnpike companies soon opened in the New England and Middle Atlantic states, but by 1825, when the Erie Canal opened, most of them had gone out of business and their stock became worthless because the tolls were insufficient to pay for their maintenance, let alone dividends to the stockholders. Since turnpikes were not practical, many entrepreneurs built canals, but these were short-lived thanks to the new railroads. This development left the towns and states to care for the now deteriorating turnpikes and their local roads.

After the Revolutionary War, a passable road had existed in Maryland between Baltimore and Cumberland, but that was as far west as one could travel safely. In 1806 President Thomas Jefferson appointed road commissioners to lay out a highway to start at Cumberland and extend to the Mississippi River. Construction began nine years later, and in 1818 the first stagecoach sped down the new highway. People soon referred to it as Uncle Sam's Pike, The National Road, or The Pike, which was misleading because there were no tollgates. By the time it reached the Mississippi River in 1840, railroads were operating in most states, and interest in highway construction had dissipated because it was thought that the speedy steam engines provided superior transportation. As a result the states and towns lost interest in maintaining their roads, which led to a period known as "the dark ages of the roads."

The appearance of horseless carriages at the turn of the twentieth century sparked a new wave of road building. Those first fragile automobiles had such difficulty coping with the muddy, rough roads that flat tires and breakdowns were frequent. Something had to be done to provide good surface conditions for these new cars coming from several factories.

Cement appeared to be the best solution, and in 1909 Wayne County, Michigan, laid a mile of cement highway. This sparked the creation of almost six hundred Good Roads associations dedicated to rebuilding and resurfacing other roads. Wealthy interests organized a company to build the Lincoln Highway from Jersey City to San Francisco. Construction began in 1914 and pushed west 3,389 miles, reaching its goal thirteen years later. In 1916 Congress started appropriating money for roads, dividing the funds among the states. At last the goal of good roads seemed possible!

## Parkways, Freeways, and Interstates

Just above the line that separates New York City from its northern neighbor, Westchester County, steam shovels were busy digging a new roadway alongside a small muddy stream called the Bronx River. It was 1906 and county officials were taking the first steps to provide good highways for the growing number of automobiles. They had decided to construct a new kind of road—a parkway—just for passenger cars.

The county had purchased a narrow fifteen-mile strip of land beside the river. They tore down old buildings, cleared out junkyards, then laid the pavement and planted grass, shrubs, and trees along each side of the road to make a park. The Bronx River Parkway was one of the first limited access roads, a highway that motorists could enter or leave at only a few places. Other cities soon built similar parkways, and back in Michigan, Wayne County constructed a new sixteen-mile limited-access highway from Detroit to Pontiac. This was not a parkway, however, but a road that went through both business and residential areas and was open to all types of traffic. But the trucks proved so noisy and annoying to people living close to the road that the highway planners realized it was not the answer for city traffic.

During the early 1930s, California adopted legislation providing for construction of freeways—limited access roads with no tolls but with trees and grass planted on both sides of the pavement, as well as fencing to prevent people and animals from crossing the roadway. Since that time many miles of wider and wider freeways have been built in California. In Texas the state highway department urged all road planners to save trees when widening or straightening roads and also to add plantings to make highways more attractive. At the same time rest stations and picnic areas were constructed.

While Californians were planning freeways and other states were building new highways, Pennsylvania residents suddenly learned that their state was going to build a turnpike and, just as in the days of the Lancaster Turnpike, charge tolls. Because the Lincoln Highway had grades of as much as 9.7 percent (one hundred feet of road rising 9.7 feet) to get over the Alleghenies, most trucks took a longer route through New York or Maryland instead.

The Pennsylvania Highway Commission formed a private company to build a new 160-mile express highway across the state. There would be two double lanes of road, one for eastbound and the other for westbound traffic, with tollbooths at each exit. There would be no crossroads, red lights, stops, or steep grades, while wide curves would permit traffic to go as fast as ninety miles per hour. The few entrances and exits would be built in the form of cloverleafs, for increased safety. Furthermore, by following the right-of-way of the South Penn Railroad, started after the Civil War but never finished, the railroad bed and its seven half-completed tunnels would save time and money.

The turnpike was completed in twenty months, a record for such construction. Motorists could make better time than the railroad, truckers used it year-round, and at last the historic land barrier between the Atlantic seaboard and the Middle West had been broken.

## U.S. Superhighway System

The largest public construction project of all time was put into motion in 1944 when Congress passed legislation to provide a National System of Interstate and Defense Highways. It called for forty-one thousand (since lengthened to more than forty-five thousand) miles of high-speed roads at a cost of $27 billion (also increased considerably). Of every dollar spent, the federal government would pay ninety cents and the state ten cents. Most of the money was to be raised by taxes on gasoline, tires, and auto hardware. The completed system would link all cities in the United States with populations over fifty thousand.

As with any project this size, there are bound to be problems, opposition, criticism, and delays. Not all Americans favored superhighways. People in large cities feared the noise, and many did not want to give up scarce open space for a four- or six-lane roadway. In many municipalities and towns, low-income residents were displaced when their property was taken for the interstates. Historical neighborhoods were sacrificed; farmers whose land was divided often lost the use of property thus made inaccessible. Parklands, wildlife, and scenic points were threatened, and noise and air pollution were common complaints.

Nevertheless, on the favorable side, superhighways have made life better for many. Interstates have pushed up property values of land lying near them, and adjacent businesses have benefited. Most people agree that as our population keeps growing, more roads are needed as well as more mass transit (buses and trains) to reduce traffic pressure in cities. Even more urgent is the need to properly maintain our huge road system, as pavement constantly needs replacing, dangerous cracks and potholes develop, bridges become unsafe, and many curves need to be reduced, to say nothing of the desirability of relocating some roads.

As of October 31, 2002, all but 5.6 miles of the 42,793-mile interstate system were completed and open to traffic in what is today called the Dwight D. Eisenhower National System of Interstate and Defense Highways, honoring President Eisenhower's commitment to the program. Not only do we have the world's finest network of safe highways but also never-ending opportunities for those seeking careers in this vital and exciting nationwide highway construction industry.

## Trans-Canada Highway System

The Trans-Canada Highway is a joint federal-provincial system that joins the ten provinces of Canada. It was approved by the Trans-Canada Highway Act of 1948, and construction began in 1950. The highway system officially opened in 1962 and was completed in 1971. Throughout much of the country, at least two routes are designated as part of the Trans-Canada Highway. In the western provinces, for example, both the main Trans-Canada route and the Yellowhead Highway are part of the system.

Unlike the American Interstate highway system, not all of the Trans-Canada Highway uses limited-access freeways, or even four-lane roads. Canada does not have a comprehensive national highway system; rather it leaves decisions about highway and freeway construction entirely to the jurisdictions of the individual provinces. In 2000 the federal government considered funding a project to convert the entire system to freeway. Although freeway construction funding was made available to some provinces, the final decision was against the conversion. Opposition to funding the freeway upgrade was mainly based on low traffic levels in parts of the Trans-Canada system; most provinces preferred to allocate the money for improving vital trade routes (often not interprovincial) and border crossings with the United States.

## Construction Laborers

Road and highway construction and maintenance require a wide range of skilled and unskilled workers from the construction industry. The majority of the work is performed by construction laborers and construction equipment operators, who work together to assemble the equipment, prepare the site, and carry out all the building functions required to construct the highway.

In highway construction, laborers are responsible for a variety of activities. They remove trees and debris; tend pumps, compressors, and generators; and build forms for pouring concrete. They also erect and disassemble scaffolding and other temporary structures. In addition, laborers tend machines; for example, they may mix concrete using a portable mixer or tend a machine that pumps concrete, grout, cement, sand, or plaster.

These workers are responsible for the installation and maintenance of traffic control devices and patterns, which may include clearing and preparing highway work zones and rights-of-way; installing traffic barricades, cones, and markers; and controlling traffic passing near, in, and around work zones. They also dig trenches; install sewer, water, and storm drain pipes; and place concrete and asphalt on roads. Other highly specialized tasks include operating laser guidance equipment to place pipes; operating air, electric, and pneumatic drills; and transporting and setting explosives for tunnel, shaft, and road construction.

The equipment that is used by laborers in highway construction includes pavement breakers; jackhammers; earth tampers; concrete, mortar, and plaster mixers; electric and hydraulic boring machines; torches; small mechanical hoists; laser-beam equipment; surveying and measuring equipment; and various other tools. They may use computers and other high-tech input devices to control robotic pipe cutters and cleaners. To perform their jobs effectively, construction laborers not only must be familiar with the duties of other craft workers, but with the materials, tools, and machinery they use as well.

## Working Conditions

Construction laborers often work as part of a team with other skilled craft workers, jointly carrying out assigned construction tasks. At other times, they may work alone, reading and interpreting instructions, plans, and specifications with very little or no supervision.

Most laborers do physically demanding work. They lift and carry heavy objects, and stoop, kneel, crouch, or crawl in awkward positions. Some work at great heights or outdoors in all weather conditions. Some jobs expose workers to harmful materials or chemicals, fumes, odors, loud noise, or dangerous machinery. To avoid injury, workers in these jobs wear safety clothing such as gloves, hard hats, protective chemical suits, and devices to protect their eyes, respiratory system, or hearing. While working in underground construction, laborers must be especially alert to safely follow procedures and must deal with a variety of hazards.

Laborers generally work eight-hour shifts, although longer shifts are common. Overnight work may be required when working on highways. Construction laborers may work only during certain seasons in certain parts of the country. They may also experience weather-related work stoppages at any time of the year.

## Job Training

Many construction laborer jobs require few skills, but others require specialized training and experience. If you enter the occupation with few skills, you can start by finding a job with a contractor who will provide on-the-job training. As an entry-level worker, you will generally start as a helper, assisting more experienced workers. Another option is assignment by a temporary help agency that sends laborers to construction sites for short-term work.

As a beginning laborer, you'll perform routine tasks such as cleaning and preparing the worksite and unloading materials. You will learn how to do more difficult tasks, such as operating tools and equipment, from experienced construction trades workers. If you are serious about advancing, you might decide to attend a trade or vocational school or a community college to receive further trade-related training.

The most skilled laborers usually have more formalized training. Some employers, particularly large nonresidential construction contractors with union membership, offer formal apprenticeships. If you are able to enroll in such a program, you would take between two and four years of classroom and on-the-job training. The first two hundred hours of your core curriculum will consist of basic construction skills such as blueprint reading, the correct use of tools and equipment, and knowledge of safety and health procedures. The remainder of the curriculum consists of specialized skills training in three of the largest segments of the construction industry: building construction, heavy/highway construction, and environmental remediation, such as lead or asbestos abatement and mold or hazardous waste remediation. Apprenticeship applicants usually must be at least eighteen years old and meet local requirements. Because the number of apprenticeship programs is limited, only a small proportion of laborers learn their trade through these programs.

High school classes in English, mathematics, physics, mechanical drawing, blueprint reading, welding, and general shop are recommended. As a laborer, you will need manual dexterity, eye-hand coordination, good physical fitness, an ability to work as a member of a team, and a good sense of balance. The ability to solve arithmetic problems quickly and accurately also is required. In addition, a good work history or military service is viewed favorably by most contractors. Computer skills also are important for advancement, as construction becomes increasingly mechanized and computerized.

## Earnings

According to the most recently available data from the Bureau of Labor Statistics, in 2004 construction laborers earned a median hourly wage of $12.10, with the majority earning between $9.47 and $16.88. For those employed in highway, street, and bridge construction, median earnings were $13.55.

Earnings for construction laborers can be reduced by poor weather or by downturns in construction activity, which sometimes result in layoffs. Apprentices or helpers usually start at about 50 percent of the wage rate paid to experienced workers. Pay increases as apprentices gain experience and learn new skills.

Some laborers belong to the Laborers' International Union of North America.

## Employment Outlook

Although employment of construction laborers is expected to grow slowly through the year 2014, job opportunities are expected to be plentiful due to the numerous openings that occur each year as laborers leave the occupation. Opportunities will be best for those with experience and specialized skills and for those willing to relocate to areas with new construction projects.

Employment of construction laborers, like that of many other construction workers, can be variable or intermittent due to the limited duration of construction projects and the cyclical nature of the construction industry. Employment opportunities can vary greatly by state and locality. During economic downturns, job openings for construction laborers decrease as the level of construction activity declines.

## Construction Equipment Operators

Construction equipment operators use machinery that moves construction materials, earth, and other heavy materials and applies asphalt and concrete to roads and other structures.

Operators control equipment by moving levers or foot pedals, operating switches, or turning dials. The operation of much of this equipment is becoming more complex as a result of computerized controls. Global Positioning System (GPS) technology also is used to help with grading and leveling. In addition to controlling the equipment, operators set up and inspect the equipment, make adjustments, and perform some maintenance and minor repairs.

Included among these workers are paving, surfacing, and tamping equipment operators; pile-driver operators; and operating engineers and other construction equipment operators. This last group of workers operates one or several types of power construction equipment. They may operate excavation and loading machines equipped with scoops, shovels, or buckets that dig sand, gravel, earth, or similar materials and load it into trucks or onto conveyors. In addition to the familiar bulldozers, they operate trench excavators, road graders, and similar equipment. Sometimes they may drive and control industrial trucks or tractors equipped with forklifts or booms for lifting materials or with hitches for pulling trailers. They also may operate and maintain air compressors, pumps, and other power equipment at construction sites. Construction equipment operators who are classified as operating engineers are capable of operating several different types of construction equipment at a site.

Paving and surfacing equipment operators use levers and other controls to operate machines that spread and level asphalt or spread and smooth concrete for roadways or other structures. Asphalt paving machine operators control valves to regulate the temperature and flow of asphalt onto the roadbed. They must see to it that the machine distributes the paving material evenly and without voids and make sure that there is a constant flow of asphalt going into the hopper. Concrete paving machine operators control levers and turn hand wheels to move attachments that spread, vibrate, and level wet concrete within forms. They use other attachments to smooth the surface of the concrete, spray on a curing compound, and cut expansion joints. Tamping equipment operators run machines that compact earth and other fill materials for roadbeds. They also may operate machines with interchangeable hammers to cut or break up old pavement and drive guardrail posts into the earth.

Pile-driver operators control large machines, mounted on skids, barges, or cranes, that hammer piles into the ground. Piles are long heavy beams of wood or steel that are necessary to support retaining walls, bulkheads, bridges, piers, or building foundations. Operators move hand and foot levers and turn valves to activate, position, and control the pile-driving equipment.

## Working Conditions

Operating construction equipment on a highway project is demanding work that goes on in nearly every type of climate and weather condition, although in many areas of the country, some operations must be suspended in winter. Also, during periods of extremely wet weather, grading and leveling activities can be difficult to perform and may be suspended. Bulldozers, scrapers, and especially tampers and pile drivers are noisy and shake or jolt the operator. This work can be dangerous, but as with most machinery, accidents generally can be avoided by observing proper operating procedures and safety practices.

Operators may have irregular hours because work on some highway construction projects continues around the clock or must be performed late at night or early in the morning.

Operators need to be in good physical condition and have a good sense of balance, the ability to judge distance, and eye-hand-foot coordination. Some operator positions require the ability to work at heights.

## *Job Training*

Although you can learn construction equipment operation skills on the job by operating light equipment under the guidance of an experienced operator and eventually advancing to heavier equipment, it is generally accepted that formal training provides more comprehensive skills. Training is available in formal apprenticeship programs that are administered by union-management committees of the International Union of Operating Engineers and the Associated General Contractors of America. Programs consist of at least three years, or six thousand hours, of on-the-job training and 144 hours a year of related classroom instruction. Because apprentices learn to operate a much wider variety of machines than do other beginners, completing such a program will often provide you with better job opportunities.

You will generally need a high school diploma to enter this field, although some employers may train nongraduates to operate some types of equipment. Technologically advanced construction equipment with computerized controls and improved hydraulics and electronics requires more skill to operate, so you may need more training and some understanding of electronics. Mechanical aptitude and high school training in automobile mechanics are helpful because you will most likely perform some maintenance on the machines. High school courses in science and mechanical drawing are also useful.

## Earnings

Earnings in this field vary. Based on currently available data, in 2004 the median hourly earnings of operating engineers and other construction equipment operators were $17.00. The majority earned between $13.19 and $23.00. For those employed in highway, street, and bridge construction, median earnings were $19.20.

The median hourly wage of paving, surfacing, and tamping equipment operators was $14.42, with most earning between $11.35 and $19.30. Those in highway construction earned $14.56. The majority of pile-driver operators earned median hourly wages ranging between $15.50 and $30.23.

## Employment Outlook

Job opportunities for construction equipment operators are certainly expected to be good through 2014, increasing between 9 and 17 percent, partly due to expected growth in highway, bridge, and street construction. Bridge construction is expected to grow the fastest, due to the need to repair or replace structures before they become unsafe. Highway conditions also will spur demand for highway maintenance and repair.

Like that of other construction workers, employment of construction equipment operators is sensitive to fluctuations in the economy. Workers may experience periods of unemployment when the level of construction activity falls.

# 3

# TRUCKING INDUSTRY

THE TRUCKING INDUSTRY offers a wonderful opportunity for those who enjoy independence and variety in their work yet appreciate the consistency and dependability of regular employment.

## History of Trucking

It might be said that the motor truck industry dates back some four thousand to six thousand years, when two-wheeled carts and then four-wheeled wagons were first built to carry goods. Pulled by horses, oxen, or other domesticated livestock, the vehicles took advantage of animal power until the development of the steam engine and then the internal combustion engine around 1900.

As we noted in Chapter 2, some three hundred years ago Indian trails winding through forests provided the first roads. Once these were widened to become a one-chop road, a horse and rider or a horse loaded with goods could travel long distances and offer a rudimentary freight service. With the development of two-chop roads, wagons replaced packhorses and made larger freight shipments possible.

As migrants from the Atlantic seaboard states made their way across the Alleghenies, shippers and businessmen formed wagon trains to transport the goods that new settlers in Pennsylvania, Ohio, and other states were anxious to purchase. The Conestoga wagon was the first efficient freight carrier and led to the introduction of the prairie schooner, a covered wagon used by those crossing the Great Plains. Since the land was flat, the absence of roads was not a serious deterrent to their passage. Those heading west traveled in groups or wagon trains for protection from Indian attacks, as did the supply wagons that serviced isolated military camps and forts.

By 1850 most of these trains had disappeared in the East, and wagons were used primarily for short-haul trips or by peddlers who called on customers in remote areas. Trains picked up most of the long-distance freight traffic, and the same transition occurred in the West once the transcontinental railroad had opened and other railroads began to crisscross the states.

When automobiles first appeared on city streets around the beginning of the twentieth century, most trucks were still horse drawn, except for a few powered by steam or electricity. By 1904 the approximately seven hundred electric- or gasoline-driven trucks in the entire United States were hardly a threat to the traditional horse and wagon. Solid rubber tires and poor springs ensured such a rough ride for these trucks on the unimproved roads that some goods were easily damaged and long-distance trips were not practical. As is still true today, batteries provided a very short range for the few electrically powered trucks.

World War I gave the trucking industry the impetus it needed, as the government awarded numerous contracts for various types of trucks to be used by the army here and abroad. Now that truck operation had become fairly reliable, pneumatic tires had replaced solid rubber, more powerful gasoline engines were available, and more roads were paved, trucks gradually took their place in both short- and long-haul cargo transportation, and their number grew to more than six hundred thousand by 1918. Finally, more than forty years later, the interstate highway system was gradually blanketing the whole nation, and trucks could compete with railroads in earnest.

## Competition for the Short-Haul Railroads

As late as the 1950s, huge train yards were busy places in the afternoon. Noisy switch engines put the long freights together so that they would be ready for their scheduled departures in the evening. Some of the faster trains received imaginative names like Red Ball Express, Overland Limited, Merchants Dispatch, or Evening Mercury. Tower workers, conductors, engineers, and dispatchers paid more attention to running these trains on schedule than they did to unprofitable passenger trains. Nevertheless, the future was not bright for the rails. The nation's forty-thousand-mile interstate highway system had been creeping over mountains, through valleys, and over rivers as it laid mile after mile of smooth four-lane roads and opened exciting new prospects for truckers both large and small.

What happened to the New York, New Haven, and Hartford Railroad in New England was typical of the times. Before the New

England Thruway (Interstate 95) opened in the late 1950s, numerous fast freights snaked their way along the heavily traveled New York–Boston Atlantic coastline route. Then with the opening of Interstate 95, which enabled trucks to roar between these two cities in four hours, more and more cargo was diverted from freight cars to trailer trucks. Lower rates and better service enticed more and more shippers to try the trucks.

Except for heavy shipments of bulk materials such as grain, coal, oil, lumber, livestock, chemicals, and liquefied gas, the railroads were forced to relinquish most of their business to the trucks. Eventually short-haul railroads like the New Haven went into bankruptcy. They then lost their identities altogether as they were forced to merge with other carriers to survive.

## Freight Categories

There are two kinds of truck freight: less than truckload (LTL) and truckload. Less than truckload refers to a cargo that is insufficient to fill a large truck. Companies that provide LTL service use smaller vehicles that make several stops to pick up enough freight to fill a larger tractor-trailer. This truck then carries its cargo to a control terminal where the packages are sorted and hauled by other trucks to terminals in various cities, where they are sorted again and put on smaller trucks for delivery.

The second category of freight, truckload, refers to a truck that picks up a complete load of goods from one shipper and hauls it directly to a single company or location in another city. Most of the new companies entering the trucking industry are interested in the truckload business because it is less expensive to operate and may be run with nonunion labor.

## Trucking Business Today

Trucking is a huge business, one of the most important in the transportation field, taking in approximately $200 billion annually and with more than fifty million trucks on the roads in the United States and five million in Canada. In the United States the industry employs more than seven million men and women, of whom almost three million are drivers. Since trucking companies are found in almost every part of the country, there is real employment opportunity for those seeking careers in this business.

Back in 1930, Galen Rousch, an attorney, and his brother, Carroll, founded a small company in Akron, Ohio, which they called Roadway Express. Today the company's headquarters are still in Akron, and it has become the number one trucker in North America, serving the United States, Canada, Mexico, and Puerto Rico. It grew by buying up smaller companies and then extending its routes throughout the country. With more than forty thousand tractors, trailers, and trucks, and nearly twenty-four thousand employees, the company takes in well over a billion dollars in revenue annually. On an average day the company delivers nearly fifty thousand shipments, which are handled through its 349 service centers.

The number one career in trucking is that of driver. Because it offers one of the more attractive and better paying jobs and does not require specialized formal education, let's first look at what is required to be a long-distance truck driver.

## Long-Distance Truck Drivers

A good proportion of long-distance truck drivers work for companies that offer services to businesses in general. Some are employees of specialized companies, such as furniture manufacturers that own and operate their own trucks. A number of drivers also own their own trucks and either operate independently, serving a number of businesses, or work under a lease arrangement to a trucking company.

In addition, industrial truck operators drive small electric-powered trucks and forklifts within industrial plants. Their vehicles haul heavy machinery, motors, parts, and other materials to and from all locations in a factory or industrial complex.

New technologies are changing the way truck drivers work, especially long-distance truck drivers. Satellites and the Global Positioning System (GPS) link many trucks with their companys' headquarters. Troubleshooting information, directions, weather reports, and other important communications can be instantly relayed to the truck, and drivers can easily communicate with the dispatcher to discuss delivery schedules and courses of action in the event of mechanical problems. The satellite link also allows the dispatcher to track the truck's location, fuel consumption, and engine performance. Some drivers also work with computerized inventory tracking equipment. It is important for the producer, warehouse, and customer to know their product's location at all times so they can maintain a high level of service.

Heavy truck and tractor-trailer drivers operate trucks or vans with a capacity of at least twenty-six thousand pounds gross vehicle weight (GVW). They transport goods including cars, livestock, and other materials in liquid, loose, or packaged form. Many routes are from city to city and cover long distances. Some companies use two drivers on very long runs, so that one can drive while the other sleeps in a berth behind the cab. These "sleeper" runs can last for days or even weeks. Trucks on sleeper runs typically stop only for fuel, food, loading, and unloading.

Some drivers who have regular runs transport freight to the same city on a regular basis. Other drivers perform ad hoc runs because shippers request varying service to different cities every day.

Long-distance heavy truck and tractor-trailer drivers spend most of their working time behind the wheel, but they may also have to load or unload their cargo. This is especially common when drivers haul specialty cargo, because they may be the only ones at the destination familiar with procedures or certified to handle the materials. Auto-transport drivers, for example, position cars on the trailers at the manufacturing plant and remove them at the dealership. When picking up or delivering furniture, drivers of long-distance moving vans hire local workers to help them load or unload.

## *Working Conditions*

Truck driving has become less physically demanding because most trucks now have more comfortable seats, better ventilation, and improved, ergonomically designed cabs. Although these changes make the work environment less taxing, driving for many hours at a stretch, loading and unloading cargo, and making many deliveries can be tiring. Design improvements in newer trucks have reduced stress and increased the efficiency of long-distance drivers. Many newer trucks are equipped with refrigerators, televisions, and bunks, which is particularly important for the many self-employed long-distance drivers who own and operate their trucks and spend most of the year away from home.

The U.S. Department of Transportation governs work hours and other working conditions of truck drivers engaged in interstate commerce. Transport Canada regulates these conditions for Canadian drivers. A long-distance driver may drive for eleven hours and work for up to fourteen hours—including driving and nondriving duties—after having ten hours off. Drivers may not drive after having worked for sixty hours in the past seven days or seventy hours in the past eight days unless they have taken at least thirty-four consecutive hours off. Drivers are required to keep a log of their activities, the condition of the truck, and the circumstances of any accidents. Many drivers, particularly on long runs, work close to the maximum time permitted because they typically are compensated according to the number of miles or hours they drive. Drivers on long runs face boredom, loneliness, and fatigue. Drivers often travel nights, holidays, and weekends to avoid traffic delays.

## Qualifications and Training

The required qualifications and standards for truck drivers are governed by state or provincial and federal regulations, and all truck drivers must comply with federal regulations and any state regulations that are in excess of those federal requirements.

To work as a long-distance truck driver, you will need a driver's license issued by your home state or province, and you will most likely have to present a clean driving record. To drive a truck designed to carry twenty-six thousand pounds or more, including most tractor-trailers and bigger straight trucks, you'll need to obtain a commercial driver's license (CDL) from the state or province in which you live. You will also need a CDL to drive any size truck transporting hazardous materials. To receive the hazardous materials endorsement, you must be fingerprinted and submit to a criminal background check by the Transportation Security Administration.

To qualify for a CDL, you must have a clean driving record, pass a written test on rules and regulations, and show that you can operate a commercial truck safely. A national database permanently records all driving violations committed by those who have a CDL, and states check these records and will deny a CDL if you have had a license suspended or revoked in another state. As a trainee, you will be accompanied by a licensed driver until you get your own CDL. Because you may not hold more than one license at a time, you'll have to surrender any other licenses when a CDL is issued. Information on how to apply for a commercial license may be obtained from state or provincial motor vehicle administrations. The United States and Canada have an agreement making the medical fitness requirements for a CDL reciprocal between the two countries.

Many states allow those who are as young as eighteen years old to drive trucks within their borders. However, the U.S. Department of Transportation (DOT) requires drivers to be twenty-one years of age in order to drive a commercial vehicle between states. Transport Canada requires long-haul drivers and those transporting goods into the United States to be at least twenty-one.

Federal motor carrier safety regulations published by the DOT require drivers to be at least twenty-one years old and to pass a physical examination once every two years. To pass the physical, you must have good hearing, at least 20/40 vision with glasses or corrective lenses, a seventy-degree field of vision in each eye, normal use of arms and legs, and normal blood pressure. The use of controlled substances other than those prescribed by a physician is prohibited. In addition, federal regulations require employers to test their drivers for alcohol and drug use as a condition of employment, and they require periodic random tests of drivers who are on duty.

You will not be allowed to drive a truck if you have been convicted of a felony involving the use of a motor vehicle, a crime involving drugs, driving under the influence of drugs or alcohol, refusing to submit to an alcohol test required by a state, leaving the scene of a crime, or causing a fatality through negligent operation of a motor vehicle. All drivers must be able to read and speak English well enough to read road signs, prepare reports, and communicate with law enforcement officers and the public.

Many trucking operations have higher standards than those described here. Some firms require that drivers be at least twenty-two years old, be able to lift heavy objects, and have driven trucks for three to five years. Many prefer to hire high school graduates and require annual physical examinations. Companies have an economic incentive to hire less risky drivers, as good drivers use less fuel and cost less to insure.

You can take driver-training courses as a way of preparing for truck driving jobs and for obtaining a CDL. High school courses in driver training and automotive mechanics also may be helpful. Many private and public vocational-technical schools offer tractor-trailer driver training programs, where you can learn to maneuver large vehicles on crowded streets and in highway traffic and to inspect trucks and freight for compliance with regulations. Some programs provide only a limited amount of actual driving experience, and completion of a program does not guarantee a job. If you are considering attending a driving school, check with local trucking companies to make sure the school's training is acceptable. Some states will require that you complete a training course in basic truck driving before issuing your CDL. The Professional Truck Driver Institute (PTDI), a nonprofit organization established by the trucking industry, manufacturers, and others, certifies driver training courses at truck driver training schools that meet industry standards and Federal Highway Administration guidelines for training tractor-trailer drivers.

Once hired, you will likely receive some training, which may consist of only a few hours of instruction from an experienced driver, sometimes on your own time. As a new driver, you may also ride with and observe experienced drivers before getting your own assignments. You will receive additional training to drive special types of trucks or handle hazardous materials. Some companies give one to two days of classroom instruction covering general duties, the operation and loading of a truck, company policies, and the preparation of delivery forms and company records.

Although most new truck drivers are assigned to regular driving jobs immediately, you may start as an extra driver, substituting for regular drivers who are ill or on vacation and receiving a regular assignment when an opening occurs. You might start on panel trucks or other small straight trucks and advance to larger, heavier trucks and finally to tractor-trailers as you gain experience and show competent driving skills.

Advancement for truck drivers generally is limited to driving runs that provide increased earnings or preferred schedules or working conditions. Some long-distance drivers buy trucks and go into business for themselves. Some of these owner-operators are successful; others fail to cover expenses and go out of business. Owner-operators should have good business sense as well as truck driving experience. Courses in accounting, business, and business mathematics are helpful. Knowledge of truck mechanics enables owner-operators to do their own routine maintenance and minor repairs.

## Wages, Hours, and Unions

Drivers who work for large trucking companies usually enjoy the highest wages. Rates of pay are fairly uniform because this occupation is strongly unionized. Union contracts are often master agreements covering all employers within a multistate region. Earnings of each driver will vary, though, depending on the number of miles he or she drives, the number of hours worked, and the type of truck driven.

According to the most recent available statistics, in 2004 median hourly earnings of heavy truck and tractor-trailer drivers were $16.11, with most earning between $12.67 and $20.09 an hour. The lowest 10 percent earned less than $10.18, and the highest 10 percent earned more than $24.07 an hour. Median hourly earnings in the industries employing the largest numbers of heavy truck and tractor-trailer drivers were:

| | |
|---|---|
| General freight trucking | $17.56 |
| Grocery and related product wholesaler | $17.32 |
| Specialized freight trucking | $15.61 |
| Employment services | $14.82 |
| Cement and concrete product manufacturing | $14.47 |

Employers pay long-distance drivers primarily by the mile. The per-mile rate can vary greatly from employer to employer and may even depend on the type of cargo being hauled. Some long-distance drivers are paid a percent of each load's revenue. Typically, earnings increase with mileage driven, seniority, and the size and type of truck driven.

Most self-employed truck drivers are engaged in long-distance hauling. Many truck drivers are members of the International Brotherhood of Teamsters. Some truck drivers employed by companies outside the trucking industry are members of unions representing the plant workers of the companies for which they work.

## Employment Outlook

Job opportunities for long-distance truck drivers are expected to be favorable over the next several years, due to economic growth and increases in the amount of freight carried by truck. Demand for long-distance drivers will remain strong because they can transport perishable and time-sensitive goods more effectively than alternate modes of transportation. Even competing forms of freight transportation, such as rail, air, and ship, require trucks to move goods between ports, depots, airports, warehouses, retailers, and final customers.

Jobs vary greatly in terms of earnings, weekly work hours, the number of nights spent on the road, and quality of equipment. There may be competition for the jobs with the highest earnings and most favorable work schedules.

Opportunities may vary from year to year, because the output of the economy dictates the amount of freight to be moved. Companies tend to hire more drivers when the economy is strong and their services are in high demand. When the economy slows, employers hire fewer drivers or may lay off some drivers. Independent owner-operators are particularly vulnerable to slowdowns. Industries least likely to be affected by economic fluctuation, such as grocery stores, tend to be the most stable employers of truck drivers and driver/sales workers.

# Local Truck Drivers

Local trucks, which operate within a city, town, or limited area, usually do the initial pickups from plants and factories and take freight to terminals where it may be consolidated with other shipments or placed directly on a long-distance truck. These same local trucks may pick up freight that has arrived at the terminal and then deliver it to stores and homes.

Light or delivery services truck drivers operate vans and trucks weighing less than twenty-six thousand pounds GVW, picking up or delivering merchandise and packages within a specific area. This may include short "turnarounds" to deliver a shipment to a nearby city, pick up another loaded truck or van, and drive it back to their home base the same day. These services may require use of electronic delivery tracking systems to track the whereabouts of the merchandise or packages. Local drivers usually load or unload the merchandise at the customer's place of business, and they may have helpers if there are many scheduled deliveries or if the load requires heavy moving. Material handlers generally load the trucks and arrange items for ease of delivery before the driver arrives at work. Customers must sign receipts for goods and pay drivers the balance due on the merchandise if there is a cash-on-delivery arrangement. At the end of the day, drivers turn in receipts, payments, records of deliveries made, and any reports on mechanical problems with their trucks.

Some local truck drivers have sales and customer service responsibilities, which are primarily to deliver and sell their firm's products over established routes or within an established territory. They sell goods such as food products, including restaurant take-out items, or pick up and deliver items such as laundry. Their response to customer complaints and requests can make the difference between a large order and a lost customer. Route drivers may also take orders and collect payments.

The trucking industry is so diversified that it is impossible to mention all the types of companies that offer career possibilities. If this business interests you, obtain a chauffeur's license and start your job search right at home by considering some of the businesses that operate their own trucks.

Some of these businesses employ drivers who are both salespeople and drivers, as in many laundry, dry cleaning, milk, and bakery businesses. Don't overlook the possibilities of a career as a driver with a fuel oil supplier who sells gasoline, bottled gas, and heating oil. A lumberyard that makes deliveries of building supplies, a road construction company that operates a fleet of trucks and other heavy equipment, a bulk milk company that delivers milk in huge stainless steel containers, and the small retail stores that operate one or more delivery trucks all could offer employment opportunities.

## Working Conditions

Local truck drivers must be skilled and able to maneuver their vehicles through dense traffic and into tight parking spaces, thread their way through narrow alleys, and expertly back up to loading platforms.

Since the trucks are used for relatively short runs, they might not be appointed with the comforts of bigger trucks used for long-distance hauling. On the positive side, unlike long-distance drivers, local drivers usually return home in the evening.

## Training and Qualifications

As is the case for long-distance drivers, local truck drivers must comply with all federal and state or provincial regulations for their profession. In many states, eighteen is the acceptable age for local drivers; some other states require drivers to be twenty-one years old. You may be required to pass an annual physical examination, exhibiting good hearing, vision, and mobility. In many states, a valid driver's license is sufficient for local truck drivers; be sure to check with the company you wish to work for to find out whether a CDL is required.

Since local drivers often deal directly with customers, you'll need to get along well with people. The ability to speak well and exhibit self-confidence, initiative, tact, and a neat appearance are also very important.

If you are hired as a driver/sales worker, you'll receive training on the various types of products the company carries so that you can answer questions about the products and market them successfully to customers.

With experience, you may advance to driving heavy or specialized trucks, or you may transfer to long-distance driving if the company also employs long-distance truck drivers.

## Earnings

According to the most current statistics available, median hourly earnings of local driver/sales workers, including commissions, were $9.66 in 2004. The majority earned between $6.94 and $14.59 an hour, while the lowest 10 percent earned less than $5.96, and the highest 10 percent earned more than $19.81 an hour. Median hourly earnings in the industries employing the largest numbers of local drivers were:

| | |
|---|---|
| Dry cleaning and laundry services | $14.67 |
| Direct selling establishments | $13.55 |
| Grocery and related produce wholesalers | $12.36 |
| Limited-service eating establishments | $6.77 |
| Full-time restaurants | $6.59 |

Most driver/sales workers receive commissions based on their sales in addition to their hourly wages.

### Employment Outlook

As with long-distance drivers, job opportunities for local truck drivers are expected to be favorable over the next few years. In fact, job opportunities for truck drivers with local carriers will be more competitive than those with long-distance carriers because of the more desirable working conditions of local carriers.

As with long-distance drivers, employment opportunities may vary based on the economy. A strong economy will lead to increases in the services that require local deliveries and the movement of goods within defined territories.

## Other Opportunities in Trucking

Truck drivers account for 45 percent of the truck transportation industry. But what about the other 55 percent of employees who aren't employed as drivers? There are many other job opportunities available in the trucking industry. We have already noted that Roadway Express employs upward of twenty-four thousand employees, but this is just one of several large trucking firms, all of which need a variety of skills to operate their various businesses successfully.

The truck on the road is like being able to see only the tip of the iceberg. To keep the trucks filled and running every day calls for a huge, coordinated, nationwide organization. The latest in management methods, computer technology, communication equipment, and automotive maintenance keeps the company going and the trucks moving.

Take Roadway Express. When a customer submits an order for a shipment to be picked up, a highly efficient system is set in motion. A trained employee takes down the details, and the minute the customer hangs up, the order is telephoned by radio to the nearest radio-controlled truck so that the driver can swing by the plant and make the pickup. As soon as the freight is loaded on the truck, the driver gives the customer an identifying number. Later, if he or she has any questions about the shipment, the information can be retrieved instantly from the computer by using this number.

While the truck is on its way to make the pickup, the pricing is being done by computer. All the necessary paperwork, such as preparing a bill of lading and the manifest, for example, are also done electronically.

The location of the truck with the recent pickup and the location of every other truck the company is operating appear on a huge map of the United States or Canada in a control center. This system enables employees to monitor every vehicle continuously and pinpoint just where any shipment is in a matter of seconds. Thanks to long-line telephone communications, all company operations are coordinated throughout the country.

As for customer relations, hundreds of representatives contact shippers and are available to help answer questions, solve problems, or assist in planning and shipping programs.

When surveying the trucking industry, let's not forget those hundreds of truck terminals, airfreight depots, and special sales offices, each staffed with personnel who handle all the clerical functions. Let's also remember the dock personnel who load and unload the trucks and sort freight, as well as the mechanics and others who service and repair the vehicles. Here is an essential business that uses workers with many skills to keep freight moving twenty-four hours a day, seven days a week.

Although the large trucking companies move much of the nation's heavy freight, there is another nationwide company that specializes in transporting only small packages, none weighing more than 150 pounds. It is probably the best-known trucker in the United States.

## Fleet of Brown Trucks

Sitting behind a desk that had once been a lunch counter, a young man was busy answering the two old-fashioned telephones that rang occasionally. His new undertaking, the American Messenger Company, consisted of the phones, two bicycles, six messengers, and himself, James Casey. It was 1907 and his basement office was located in downtown Seattle.

The messengers had to be courteous and neat to impress Mr. Casey and qualify for a job. They delivered papers and articles for local businesses and individuals in the Seattle area and were occasionally called upon to walk dogs or to carry an elderly woman's groceries.

Business was not brisk, but gradually the tiny enterprise grew. Casey changed the name to Merchants Parcel Delivery in 1913. At the same time he bought his first horseless carriage, a Model-T Ford. A year later seven motorcycles were added, and soon Merchants was handling all the deliveries for three of the largest department stores in the Seattle area.

In 1919 the company opened an office in Oakland, California, and changed its named to United Parcel Service, at the same time adopting the official UPS color, brown. Other "firsts" followed, such as the first brown uniforms for drivers, the first substation in Long Beach, California, and the first conveyor belt, which was 180 feet long and made handling packages more efficient.

It seemed that nothing could stop the growth of this dynamic company. UPS service was extended to every major West Coast city. Then the first brown trucks started rolling on New York City streets on July 14, 1930, and by year-end the fleet was delivering all parcels for 123 stores. Soon people in Midwestern states were seeing the brown trucks, and today the company serves not only the United States but more than two hundred countries and territories worldwide. In 1953 the management decided to extend UPS service beyond businesses to anyone who wanted to ship a parcel.

The secret of UPS's success is consolidating packages at every point from pickup to delivery. This system enables the company to deliver the maximum number of packages in the minimum amount of time and number of miles. The small package shipments are fed into one highly specialized system, which starts in the package car as the driver delivers packages and at the same time picks up those articles ready for shipment.

All these packages are then consolidated at the nearest center with those picked up by other drivers. Tractor-trailer units feed the packages from surrounding centers into a hub facility each night, where they are sorted and loaded into outgoing feeder vehicles that will take them to the UPS facility closest to their destination.

An equal amount of attention is given to the loading of each delivery truck. By the time each driver arrives for work, he or she finds that other workers have loaded the truck in the proper sequence so that deliveries can be made as quickly as possible over the most direct route.

No matter how remote the address of either the shipper or the receiver, UPS pick-up and delivery service is available, and each package is delivered directly to the door of the consignee. In addition, the company maintains customer counters at each of its operating locations throughout the world, and this is where individuals and business shippers can bring their packages rather than have them picked up.

As you may well imagine, this nationwide service depends on people: the men and women who answer the telephones and take your orders for pickups, the information specialists who maintain the website where you can place and track orders, the drivers who deliver and pick up the packages, the sorters at the various facilities, the drivers of the huge tractor-trailers that carry the packages long distances between centers and hubs, the pilots and crews of the airplanes that transport packages, the maintenance people who keep the trucks and planes clean and in top operating condition, the various clerical people in the offices, and the supervisory and administrative staff—all help keep UPS going.

By 2006 UPS had grown to become an international shipping giant, employing 348,400 people in the United States and another 58,000 in more than two hundred countries and territories around the world. The company maintains a fleet of more than 91,700 ground vehicles and 268 jet aircraft (making it the ninth-largest airline in the world).

Keep in mind that UPS is only one package delivery service. Federal Express and DHL have grown into equally large international corporations, each serving more than two hundred countries with a fleet of ground vehicles and airplanes to rival that maintained by UPS. You can find detailed information about each company and its career opportunities by visiting its website.

## Local and Long-Distance Movers

Another large segment of the trucking industry is devoted to moving. These companies transport furniture, pianos, and other household goods.

Back in 1891 two brothers living in Sioux City, Iowa, obtained a large cart and a strong horse and lettered the side of the wagon: "Bekins, Moving & Storage." John and Martin Bekins had very little money but lots of ambition and a sincere interest in each customer's individual needs.

One hundred years later, Bekins had grown to become the largest moving and storage company in the world, with more than four hundred locations in the United States and Canada and operations in more than one hundred foreign countries. The company claims that the brothers' original spirit has been sustained and that personal service is still the cornerstone of the business, even though the company handles more than nine hundred moves each day.

This may seem like an astronomical number of moves for just one company, but perhaps it is not so surprising when you consider that about forty million Americans, or a fifth of the population, move each year. It is the moving and storage industry that makes it possible for families to pack up and make moves of hundreds or thousands of miles, with every detail surrounding the move anticipated and efficiently handled.

Furniture movers employed by interstate companies often work in crews of three or four, one of whom is the driver who also loads and unloads along with the other movers. If one of the helpers is qualified to drive the truck, it may be possible for the van to make an uninterrupted long-distance trip. Such movers may be away from home for weeks at a time. They lead irregular lives with sixty hours of work being considered a normal workweek.

Ability to read, write, and do arithmetic; a strong back; good coordination; a sense of responsibility; and a willingness to be helpful and courteous are the main personal requirements for this job. Each driver must hold a Class I driver's license for the kind of equipment he or she will be driving. Many companies give their employees training in both packing and driving.

The majority of furniture movers work for local companies that do short-haul or local moving and also act as agents for interstate and international movers. The large moving companies have their own movers who may travel throughout the country as they transport several loads before returning to their regular terminal.

As the population continues to grow and people keep changing homes, the demand for movers should increase somewhat. Promotion to the position of estimator is possible for a mover. This person determines the weight and cost of shipping a houseful of furniture. A mover with a thorough knowledge of the business might be considered for promotion to dispatcher. The dispatcher is responsible for routing all the trucks and keeping in touch with all the drivers.

In addition to the usual clerical positions, there are openings for billing clerks, claims adjusters, maintenance workers, mechanics, and administrative personnel.

A word of warning: the moving business is a seasonal one. The busiest time is during the summer months of June, July, August, and September when children are not in school. The last week of each month is usually the busiest time.

# 4

# Evolution of Mass Transit

Imagine for a moment you are waiting on the corner for a bus to take you to school or work. It's snowing and you stamp your feet to keep from freezing. At last the bus comes, the door opens, and you can feel the welcome warmth. Seconds later you settle back in a comfortable seat and relax.

Now go back in time. It is 1716 and you are on a wagon with only a cloth or wooden roof for protection from the elements. You are one of twelve passengers sitting on four benches (without backs). The horses plod along at four miles an hour on the snowy roadway, making the 170-mile trip an endless nightmare that is broken only by infrequent stops at stages (rest stations) along the way.

More comfortable, enclosed stagecoaches with crude strap springs, as pictured in history books, did not appear until later. Although the ride was jolting and jarring, at least stagecoaches offered protection from bad weather for the fortunate passengers riding inside.

The first predecessor of today's mass transit commenced service when a six-passenger hackney coach offered short rides within New York City's Bowery. By 1830 large vehicles called *omnibuses* (from the Latin "for all") made their way up and down Manhattan. Some twenty years later, rails were laid in the streets and "horsecars," which resembled railroad coaches pulled by horses, replaced the lumbering omnibuses. The resulting ride was much smoother, faster, and easier for the horses.

As early as 1873, cable cars were introduced in several cities, using steam engines to power the underground cable apparatus. However, these were expensive to build, and several inventors were working to perfect motors large enough to propel cars by using electric power from overhead or underground wires. In 1888 Frank J. Sprague successfully operated trolleys in Richmond, Virginia, and showed they were both economical to run and strong enough to carry a full load of passengers, even up grades. Within twenty years many cities had elaborate streetcar systems, and by 1915 trolleys were running over forty-five thousand miles of tracks.

Subsequently, trolley service expanded from downtown metropolitan areas out to rural areas later called suburbs. This enabled cities to expand as the first housing projects started rising near the newly laid tracks.

## Public Transit

At the start of the twentieth century, it was possible to travel between New York and Boston by electric trolley, if you had the time and the patience to make the innumerable changes required. What's more, it was said that one might go most of the way from New York to Chicago via local trolleys and interurban lines. It was a time when trolley fever gripped the entire country, and even small towns laid single-track lines with turnouts every so often to permit cars to pass.

Trolleys took commuters to work, housewives to market, the wealthy to the opera, children to school, and vacationers to amusement parks or sparkling lakes. As long as there were passengers to fill the seats of the swaying cars, this was a relatively inexpensive, safe, and dependable way to travel.

The trolley eventually gave way to the automobile, and once the public had discovered the convenience of owning one, many people gradually abandoned the trolley, especially in small towns. Later, the development of bigger buses for use in cities and large towns provided greater convenience and safety for passengers. They could board or leave the vehicles at the curb rather than in the middle of the street where trolley tracks had to be located. Then trackless trolleys were developed to give the trolley cars greater flexibility, but the cars still had to draw current from overhead wires that were supported by unsightly poles.

As cities grew, trolleys were unable to handle the growing number of passengers traveling into and within urban areas. Subways were dug to supplement the surface transportation. Today, although trolleys have disappeared altogether from New York and many other cities, you can ride one in Boston, where they are still used, along with buses and subway trains within a coordinated transit system.

America's most unusual trolley cars are undoubtedly San Francisco's, which are as much a part of that city as the steep hills for which their endless cables and quaint cars were constructed. The cars are not the most efficient form of transportation, but they are invaluable as a tourist attraction for the city.

## Light Rail Transit

The trolley is not entirely a thing of the past. It is making a comeback in a slightly different form from earlier versions. One of the first new lines, the "Tijuana Trolley," opened in July 1981. It travels on sixteen miles of abandoned track and right-of-way between San Diego, California, and the Mexican border.

Fourteen electric trolley cars were expected to carry 10,000 riders a day as they made their eighteen stops along the way, but management was amazed when some 11,500 passengers clamored to board the cars. Soon their number grew to more than 18,000. The line proved so successful that another seventeen-mile trolley line was planned for the benefit of residents living in San Diego's eastern suburbs.

Far to the east, in Buffalo, New York, a 6.4-mile light rail system with fourteen stations pushed out from downtown to the State University of New York campus, the first part of an ambitious multiphase plan.

To the north, the Edmonton Light Rail Transit system (commonly called the LRT), is a 12.3-kilometer route that starts in the city's northeast suburbs and currently ends near the University of Alberta Hospital on the south side, with stops at eleven stations. Construction of the southern extension is under way.

In Miami, Metrorail carries passengers in air-conditioned, stainless steel trains on an elevated railway over a 21.5-mile route from south of the city to north Miami-Dade. It provides connections to all major areas of the city. With the completion of the downtown Metromover, Miami-Dade County became the first community in the world to have a people mover connected to a rail system. The Metromover is a free service that is made up of individual motorized cars running atop a 4.4-mile elevated track, looping around the downtown and connecting to the Metrorail.

Subways are not a thing of the past either. In the 1960s San Francisco built its extensive Bay Area Rapid Transit (BART) system. Atlanta opened the first 7.1 miles of its projected 53-mile MARTA system in September 1979. But the most ambitious new subway opened its first 4.6 miles of track on March 29, 1976, when the Washington (DC) Metropolitan Area Transit Authority dispatched its first train on what would eventually be a 98-mile system. Here, as in San Diego, the public's response exceeded all expectations. Some twenty-one thousand passengers were boarding at the five stations of the planned eighty-six-station system, a number that was well over the initially anticipated eight thousand passengers.

In 1900 New York City broke ground for what would become its world-famous subway system. Today, the New York subway consists of a total of 842 track miles which, if laid end to end, would reach from New York to Chicago.

Subways provide only part of essential transport services because surface transportation is also vital to the needs of travelers. Much of the urban and suburban transport service is provided by buses. Yet we should not overlook the trolleys, subways, and light rail trains that are also important to any transit system. The light rail trains operate principally in a limited-stop service, such as is offered in San Diego or Buffalo.

The introduction of computers and other automatic devices by the newer transit systems is making these organizations most interesting places to work. A brief look at the Washington Metro system will suggest a few of the innovations that are making some transit careers so intriguing.

# Washington Metro

The Washington Metro was established in 1966 to plan, construct, finance, and provide for the operation of a rapid rail and bus transit system for the Washington metropolitan area. It was to be managed by elected officials from the District of Columbia, Maryland, and Virginia.

From the very beginning, it was decided that the bus and rail systems would complement, not compete with, each other. Buses would take riders into outlying Metro stations.

As the rail system continues to expand, the bus routes are coordinated with it. The local governments whose representatives manage the Metro set the level of bus service in their areas, deciding where and how often the buses run and thus determining how much or how little they want to provide their taxpayers. Today the Metro operates the second-largest rail transit system and fifth-largest bus network in the country.

## Metrobus

The Metrobus system, which operates a fleet of more than fourteen hundred buses, complements the rail service with its four hundred basic bus routes and some eight hundred route variations. For fiscal year 2007, the Transit Authority has approved the addition of twenty-five buses that run on compressed natural gas (CNG). Between 2008 and 2012, authorization has been granted for the addition of a hundred hybrid buses each year. All of the buses are equipped with two-way radios, silent radio alarms, flashing lights for protection, and automatic vehicle locators.

In the communications center, radio dispatchers are constantly on duty providing two-way communication with each Metrobus operating in the region. This enables the dispatcher to adjust quickly to any unexpected crisis, such as an accident. A silent alarm built into the radio system enables police to respond to an operator's signal for help.

The system has modern bus garages for the storage, maintenance, and repair of its vehicles. Most of these are located in the outer suburbs to give more efficient service to Maryland and Virginia passengers, because many of the bus lines act as feeders into the Metro trains.

## Metrorail

The Metrorail system uses nearly one thousand train cars, traveling over a total of 106.3 miles of track. It takes pride in its communication and security features, which provide the highest available level of comfort and safety for passengers and employees. Train operators and the operations control center communicate by two-way radio. Hotlines are in place from the control center to police and fire departments, and an automated electronic fire protection system operates in stations and tunnels. There are chemical detection systems in underground stations.

There are fire extinguishers on platforms and in rail cars, and call boxes are placed every eight hundred feet along the tracks. Also, passenger-to-station-manager intercoms are on platforms, in elevators, and on landings, and there are passenger-to-operator intercoms at each end of the rail cars.

Control room supervisors, having an electronic overview of the entire Metro system, make and implement decisions to keep it running smoothly. The operations control center, located in the Metro headquarters building, is the hub of the vast Metro communications and control network.

Control room supervisors perform three major tasks: taking corrective action as problems occur, dispatching repair crews for equipment malfunctions or failures, and performing emergency communications. When trains fail to move as they should, the supervisors choose and execute a solution after considering a list of options. When a malfunction occurs, they know whom to call to fix it.

Train control supervisors operate two push-button consoles, one for train operations and the other for Metro support systems. The supervisor at the train operations console monitors and controls train movement. The supervisor at the other console handles problems with support systems, such as the electrical substations, station air-conditioning, tunnel ventilation, drainage, station fire and intrusion alarms, and other facilities.

The train operations supervisor uses CRT screens as electronic windows to view schematic representations of tracks, trains, and stations throughout the Metro system. Displays on the screen show tracks, crossovers, turnouts, pocket tracks, stations, and moving trains.

## Transit Tech

If a transit career interests you, inquire about possible transit tech courses in your local vocational/technical schools. In 1986 "Transit Tech" was instituted in New York City, and 400 students applied to the High School of Transit Technology. Today called East New York Transit Technology High School (H.S. 615), the school has an enrollment of 1,750 students in grades nine through twelve.

Transit Tech teaches students to repair buses and subway cars, while providing the academic background that they need for college. Many graduates go directly to work, but the academics are strong enough that some go on to four-year state and city colleges as well as private schools and universities. Some graduates even return to teach at the school.

In the "railcar lab"—which may be the largest high school classroom in the United States—students learn how to use hand tools, do lighting jobs, and do other types of work on two real subway cars. In addition to the well-equipped shops for electronics and transit technology, the school has six state-of-the-art computer labs. In fact, most majors in the school involve computers. Among these majors are computer science, computer-assisted machine technology, computer electronics, computer/industrial electrician, and computer-assisted engineering. Computer science students work as interns at the Metropolitan Transportation Authority. A dozen or so graduates per year go directly into an apprenticeship program at the MTA. An open house for prospective students is held in October.

In recent years, Transit Tech has attracted an increasing number of female students. The school keeps class size capped at twenty-seven for freshman; math classes are even smaller. It also has a strong special education program that integrates students with learning disabilities—including those whose first language is Spanish—into regular classrooms with two teachers and an extra-small class size.

## Canadian Urban Transit Association

As the representative of public transit in Canada, the Canadian Urban Transit Association (CUTA) is involved in a variety of activities in support of its mission and goals. These include conferences, training, public affairs, awards, exhibitions, technical services, research, statistics, and government relations.

CUTA was originally founded in Montréal in December 1904 as the Canadian Street Railway Association. In 1913 it became known as the Canadian Electric Railway Association. In 1932 the name was changed to Canadian Transit Association, and the present name was adopted in 1973, when the association was incorporated in its current form. The celebration of the association's centennial in 2004 was a major milestone in its history.

CUTA employs experienced staff, most of whom are transit specialists with expertise in transit planning, operations, marketing, technology, training, human resources, and policy. A broad network of national and international contacts and the association's continuing work on committees and with affiliated organizations make CUTA an authority in public transit technical and policy issues.

The majority of urban transit systems in Canada are members of CUTA. Membership includes 120 transit systems, 15 government agencies (federal, provincial, and municipal), 250 business members (the firms or persons engaged in the manufacture or sale of transit equipment or services) including consultants, and 50 affiliates. For information about CUTA's services and career opportunities, visit www.cutaactu.ca.

## Subway and Streetcar Operators

Although bus drivers might make up the majority of transit drivers, let's not forget those workers who operate the subways and streetcars in mass transit systems. Here is a look at their careers.

### Subway Operators

Subway operators control trains that transport passengers through cities and their suburbs. The trains run in underground tunnels, on the surface, or on elevated tracks. Operators must stay alert to observe signals along the track that indicate when they must start, slow, or stop their train. They also make announcements to riders, may open and close the doors of the train, and ensure that passengers get on and off the subway safely.

To meet predetermined schedules, operators must control the train's speed and the amount of time spent at each station. Increasingly, however, these functions are controlled by computers and not by the operator. During breakdowns or emergencies, operators contact their dispatcher or supervisor and may have to evacuate cars.

### Streetcar Operators

Streetcar operators drive electric-powered streetcars, trolleys, or light-rail vehicles that transport passengers around metropolitan areas. Some tracks may be recessed in city streets or have grade crossings, so operators must observe traffic signals and cope with car and truck traffic. Operators start, slow, and stop their cars so that passengers may get on and off with ease. They may collect fares and issue change and transfers, and they also answer questions from passengers concerning fares, schedules, and routes.

### Training

You will need at least a high school education for most subway and streetcar operator jobs. In a transit system that also operates buses, it's likely that you would first have worked as a bus driver before moving on to subway or streetcar operation.

You must be in good health, have good communication skills, and be able to make quick, responsible judgments. As a new operator, you will complete a training program that will last from a few weeks to six months. At the end of the classroom and on-the-job training, you must pass qualifying examinations covering the operating system, troubleshooting, and evacuation and emergency procedures. After gaining sufficient seniority, you might qualify to advance to station manager or another supervisory position.

## Earnings

Most railroad workers are paid according to miles traveled or hours worked, whichever leads to higher earnings. Full-time employees have steadier work, more regular hours, increased opportunities for overtime work, and higher earnings than do those assigned to the "extra" board.

Median hourly earnings for subway and streetcar operators were $23.70 in 2004. Approximately eight out of ten railroad transportation workers are members of unions. Many different railroad unions represent all the various crafts on the railroads. Many subway operators are members of the Amalgamated Transit Union, while others belong to the Transport Workers Union of North America.

## Other Transit Jobs

Next to driving occupations, probably the largest number of jobs will be found in the maintenance and repair shops of buses, trolleys, and subways. All vehicles must be kept in top running condition, and because most of them are used practically every day, they require frequent checks and maintenance. They are also taken out of service periodically for major repairs. All this work is usually performed by employees of the transit companies.

Cleaners, mechanics, electricians, welders, painters, upholsterers, and glaziers are some of the specialists needed to keep a fleet of transit buses and trains moving. The best way to prepare for such openings is to take special training at a trade school.

In most cities, such as in New York City, transit service operates late into the evening or all night. As a new worker, you will probably be assigned to the night or late shift. As you get seniority, you will be able to bid for better and perhaps more regular working hours.

In the office of any transit company you will find the usual clerical, computer, and receptionist positions. In addition, there are those posts that call for specialized or college training. You will find such positions in the sales, purchasing, public relations, planning, finance, and budget departments. Although turnover in these administrative offices is not likely to be high, investigate the opportunities anyway.

### Advantages and Disadvantages

Here are some reasons why you should enter this field, if it interests you:

• Most jobs are open to everyone because they are under your local municipal or other civil service system. This means that all people are guaranteed equal consideration for positions, without discrimination.

• There are good chances for promotion because many of these systems are large. Those who have college degrees and/or many years of experience may be in line for promotion to supervisory and managerial posts.

• Benefits are greater than in many other fields. The overtime, pensions, sick leave, health care, and paid vacations are more generous than in most industries.

• There is better than average job security, especially after you have been on the job several years.

On the other hand, every job has its drawbacks, and you should be prepared to face these possible disadvantages:

• Your income will rise slowly from year to year because every job is paid according to an established salary scale.

• You may work under great pressure and difficult conditions, especially when accidents, breakdowns, storms, or other problems cause the whole system to slow down or cease operating altogether.

• Public transportation operates seven days a week in most places and in some cities around the clock. Therefore you can expect that the chances are good you will have to work shifts.

• Being a public transportation employee or public servant can subject you to unpopularity, because many people think that transport workers do not work hard enough, are paid too much, and receive too many benefits.

For further information about job openings, contact your state employment security office, the public transit authority, or the municipal civil service office. If you need additional information, contact the American Public Transit Association at www.apta.com.

## Local Bus Transit

Most experienced drivers have regularly scheduled runs, but new drivers are usually placed on an "extra" list to substitute for regular drivers who are ill or on vacation. They may also be assigned to extra and special runs, perhaps during morning or evening rush hours, or to stadiums when there are special sporting events. In some cities or towns, transit buses transport schoolchildren to and from school, and extra-list drivers may operate these buses. New drivers remain on the extra list until they have enough seniority to get a regular run, which may take several years. Senior drivers may bid for the runs that they prefer, such as those with more work hours, lighter traffic, or weekends off.

Local-transit bus drivers report to their assigned terminal or garage, where they stock up on tickets or transfers and prepare trip report forms. In some transportation firms, maintenance departments are responsible for keeping vehicles in good condition; in others, drivers may be expected to check their vehicle's tires, brakes, windshield wipers, lights, oil, fuel, and water supply before beginning their routes. Drivers usually verify that the bus has safety equipment, such as fire extinguishers, first aid kits, and emergency reflectors.

During the course of their shifts, bus drivers collect fares; answer questions about schedules, routes, and transfer points; and sometimes announce stops. Intercity bus drivers may make only a single one-way trip to a distant city or a round-trip each day. They may stop at towns just a few miles apart or only at large cities hundreds of miles apart. Local-transit bus drivers may make several trips each day over the same city and suburban streets, stopping as frequently as every few blocks.

Local-transit drivers submit daily trip reports with a record of trips, significant schedule delays, and mechanical problems. Intercity drivers who drive across state or national boundaries must comply with U.S. Department of Transportation regulations. These include completing vehicle inspection reports and recording distances traveled and the periods they spend driving, performing other duties, and off duty.

## Working Conditions

Driving a bus through heavy traffic while dealing with passengers is more stressful and fatiguing than physically strenuous. Many drivers enjoy the opportunity to work without direct supervision, with full responsibility for their bus and passengers. To improve working conditions and retain drivers, many bus lines provide ergonomically designed seats and controls for drivers. Many companies use Global Positioning Systems to help dispatchers manage their bus fleets and help drivers navigate.

Regular local-transit bus drivers usually have a five-day workweek; Saturdays and Sundays are considered regular workdays. Some drivers work evenings and after midnight. To accommodate commuters, many work split shifts, for example, 6:00 A.M. to 10:00 A.M. and 3:00 P.M. to 7:00 P.M., with time off in between.

## Training

Many employers prefer high school graduates and require a written test of ability to follow complex bus schedules. For many public transit bus companies, though, you might have to be at least twenty-four years of age; and some companies require several years of experience driving a bus or a truck.

Because bus driver qualifications and standards are established by state and federal regulations, you will have to comply with federal regulations and with any state regulations that exceed federal requirements. To meet federal standards, you must hold a commercial driver's license (CDL) with the appropriate endorsements from the state in which you live. The requirements for a CDL are covered in Chapter 3 under the section "Long-Distance Truck Drivers."

If you work for a local-transit system, you will most likely be given two to eight weeks of classroom and behind-the-wheel instruction. In the classroom, you will learn Department of Transportation and company work rules, safety regulations, state and municipal driving regulations, and safe driving practices. You'll also learn to read schedules, determine fares, keep records, and deal courteously with passengers.

During training, you will practice driving on set courses. You'll practice turns and zigzag maneuvers, backing up, and driving in narrow lanes, followed by driving in light traffic and, eventually, on congested highways and city streets. You will also make trial runs without passengers to improve your driving skills and learn the routes, memorizing and driving each of the runs operating out of your assigned garage. As a new driver, you'll make regularly scheduled trips with passengers, accompanied by an experienced driver who gives helpful tips, answers questions, and evaluates your performance. Most bus drivers get brief supplemental training at regular periods to keep abreast of safety issues and regulatory changes.

Opportunities for promotion are generally limited. However, experienced drivers may become supervisors or dispatchers, where they assign buses to drivers, check whether drivers are on schedule, reroute buses to avoid blocked streets or other problems, and dispatch extra vehicles and service crews to scenes of accidents and breakdowns. In transit agencies with rail systems, drivers may become train operators or station attendants. Opportunities exist for bus drivers to become either instructors of new bus drivers or master-instructors who train new instructors. A few drivers become managers. Promotion in publicly owned bus systems is often determined by a competitive civil service examination.

## Earnings

Median hourly earnings of transit bus drivers were $14.30 in 2004, based on the most recently available statistics. The majority earned between $10.74 and $19.31. Median hourly earnings in the industries employing the largest numbers of transit bus drivers were:

| | |
|---|---|
| Local government | $17.10 |
| Interurban and rural transportation | $15.86 |
| Urban transit systems | $13.49 |

Wages for bus drivers in Canada vary depending on employer and location. Transit drivers may earn from $9 to $19 per hour; school-bus drivers may earn $10 per hour or $30 to $50 per day.

The benefits bus drivers receive from their employers also vary greatly. Most local-transit bus drivers receive paid health and life insurance, sick leave, vacation leave, and free bus rides on any of the regular routes of their line or system. Many are members of the Amalgamated Transit Union. Local-transit bus drivers in New York and several other large cities belong to the Transport Workers Union of America. Bus drivers in Canada are represented by the Amalgamated Transit Union Canada or Union of Canadian Transportation Workers. Some drivers belong to the United Transportation Union or to the International Brotherhood of Teamsters.

## Employment Outlook

Opportunities for transit bus drivers are expected to be plentiful over the next several years, although there will be competition for jobs in higher paying public transit positions. Those applicants with good driving records and who are willing to work a part-time or irregular schedules probably will have the best job prospects.

## Long-Distance Bus Transit

Long-distance buses provide many communities with their only means of public transportation to and from other areas. Those who live in large cities may find that the bus is a convenient alternative to air and rail travel. In fact, over short distances, such as between Boston and Providence, or New York and Philadelphia, the bus may prove almost as fast as a plane or train, and the service may be more frequent. Bus terminals are usually located in the heart of the city, whereas the railroad station may not be as convenient. In addition, there are those bus lines that provide intrastate service (operate wholly within one state) and companies that offer charter or other special services to the public.

Unlike other forms of transportation, which need to maintain stations or terminals with a number of workers at each stop where passengers board or leave their planes or trains, buses are uniquely able to eliminate this expense in most of the communities they serve. The corner garage, drugstore, or newsstand serves as a waiting room for passengers, and the owner sells tickets and provides travel information. These arrangements cut down on the number of employees required to operate a rural bus system.

Aside from drivers, employment opportunities would be mostly for clerical positions, some ticket agents, mechanics to service and repair the vehicles, cleaners, and perhaps a few custodians if the bus line operates its own terminal. Openings will vary according to the size of a company and the complexity of its operations. The very largest operators might offer additional employment possibilities for dispatchers, computer specialists, accountants, and applicants with an economics and/or statistical background. These last two specialties might qualify applicants as forecasters, rate and schedule specialists, and financial analysts. So-called professionals, public relations specialists, attorneys, and business librarians would find little or no real opportunities in this area.

Since the business of transporting passengers by bus is uncomplicated, a small company can operate profitably with a half dozen buses, a few drivers, and as many other employees as needed to keep the books, sell tickets, and service the vehicles. For most companies it is a "bus and driver" business. The driver is the most important employee in the business because he or she is the operator of the bus, and to the passenger that person is the company. Almost 60 percent of Greyhound's employees are drivers; therefore, if you would like to enter this industry and you enjoy driving, give careful consideration to the possibility of becoming a driver.

## Job Description

You have completed your training and are proudly wearing your new uniform as a driver, an important member of the company team. What would you do on the first day you report for work?

Upon arriving at the garage or terminal where you are assigned a bus, you pick up tickets, report forms, and other items needed for your trip. Then you find your bus and inspect the vehicle to make certain that everything is working properly. You also check the fuel, water, oil, and tires and see that the necessary safety equipment is on board.

Your inspection completed, you drive to the loading dock, and if there is no porter to help load the baggage, you stand near the door to collect tickets, check bags, and store them in the luggage compartment. You might use the terminal's public address system to announce the destination, route, time of departure and arrival at the next stop, and other information. At departure time you settle into your seat, turn on the ignition switch, and go.

If yours is a local run, you'll probably stop at many small towns only a few miles apart. At each stop you help passengers leave and board the bus, unload and load baggage, and take tickets. If it is an express run, you will probably drive several hours on an interstate or other highway before making your first stop. En route you will regulate the lighting, heating, and air-conditioning equipment. Should you get a flat or something goes wrong with the engine, it is your job to change the tire and, possibly, fix the motor, if repair service is not available.

At your destination, you discharge your passengers, drive the bus to the garage or turn it over to the next driver, and then prepare your reports. The U.S. Department of Transportation requires drivers to keep a record of each trip. The record includes distance traveled, periods of time off duty, and time spent performing other duties. You also must report any repairs or special servicing the bus might need, and it is possible that your employer expects you to complete certain company reports as well.

If you drive a chartered bus, you pick up a group of people, take them to whatever destination is set on the schedule, and remain with them until they are ready to return. Some charter buses are used for organized tours, in which case you would stay away from home for one or more nights.

Should you drive an intercity bus, you can expect to work at all hours of the day and night, every day of the year. As a new driver, you will be on call at all hours and may have to report for work on short notice. If you are away from home overnight, there will be a meal allowance and possibly reimbursement of your hotel expense. Driving schedules range from six to ten hours a day and from three and a quarter to six days a week, but under U.S. Department of Transportation regulations you cannot, as an intercity driver, drive more than ten hours without at least eight consecutive hours off. Although driving is not physically difficult, it is tiring and calls for steady nerves. You alone are responsible for the safety of your passengers and bus, and that calls for an alert mind.

## Qualifications and Training

Here are the requirements the Greyhound Corporation (which is profiled later) expects applicants to meet to work as its bus drivers. The requirements of most bus companies will be similar:

- Be at least twenty-two years of age
- Pass a U.S. DOT physical exam, criminal background check, and drug screening
- Possess a valid driver's license
- Have a good driving record (no more than two moving violations in the past three years or three violations in the past five years)
- Successfully complete the company's seven-week driver training program

Greyhound's driver training program consists of three phases. In phase one, you will have two weeks to complete twenty hours of computer-based training, which can be scheduled at your convenience. If you are selected to move on to phase two, you will attend two weeks of behind-the-wheel training in Atlanta, Georgia, Richmond, Virginia, or Reno, Nevada. Greyhound will provide lodging, meals, and a student per diem allowance during this phase. In phase three, you'll complete your training at your hiring location, where you will spend three weeks learning driving routes with a driving mentor. Your per diem will continue during this phase.

You can visit the company's website at www.greyhound.com to learn about job opportunities.

## Earnings

Based on the most recently available statistics, in 2004 median weekly earnings of bus drivers who worked full-time were $572; the majority earned between $430 and $772 a week. Bus drivers employed in interurban and rural transportation earned median hourly wages of $15.86; those working in the charter bus industry earned $10.81.

Motor coach drivers in Canada either earn an hourly wage, a wage per kilometer, or a flat fee for tours and special charters.

Most intercity drivers are represented by unions such as the Amalgamated Transit Union, the United Transportation Union, the Union of Canadian Transportation Employees, or the International Brotherhood of Teamsters.

## Employment Outlook

Local bus service feeding into large cities where passengers can connect with long-distance carriers should be on the increase, because it can be operated with small and relatively inexpensive equipment. This would spread career opportunities throughout many areas and brighten job prospects for those interested in this vital transportation service.

Most growth in intercity bus transportation will occur in group charters to locations not served by other modes of transportation.

Like automobiles, buses have a far greater number of possible destinations than airplanes or trains. Since they offer greater cost savings and convenience over automobiles, buses usually are the most economical option for tour groups traveling to out-of-the-way areas.

Full-time bus drivers rarely are laid off during recessions. If the number of passengers decreases, however, employers might reduce the hours of part-time local-transit and intercity bus drivers because fewer extra buses would be needed. Seasonal layoffs are common. Many intercity bus drivers with little seniority, for example, are furloughed during the winter, when regularly scheduled and charter business declines, and school-bus drivers seldom work during the summer or school holidays.

### Greyhound Lines

If you have a good atlas, look for the mining town of Hibbing, Minnesota, in the northeastern part of the state. Aside from being the childhood home of Bob Dylan, Hibbing's chief claim to fame is probably that it is the birthplace of the giant Greyhound Corporation, which today serves more than thirty-one hundred destinations across North America.

In 1914, horse-drawn vehicles provided most of the transportation in Hibbing, except for a few livery autos that were rented at five dollars an hour. Carl Wickman, who had recently emigrated from Sweden, owned one of the delivery cars. He had opened an auto agency, but when his one car didn't sell, he had to do something with it, so he put it out to hire.

Recognizing that people regularly traveled back and forth between Hibbing and nearby Alice, Wickman decided to operate his car hourly on a regular schedule between the two towns. He made a sign and started his little one-man, one-vehicle, bus line. The fare was fifteen cents one way, twenty-five cents round-trip. Soon passengers not only filled the car but clung to the running boards and fenders.

Being a good businessman, Wickman suggested a partnership with his only competitor, Ralph Bogan. By joining forces, they combined their capital and equipment and kept from hurting either of their enterprises. Soon they were building more buses and extending their operations south, until they reached as far as the city of Minneapolis.

As the partners were pushing their little bus line farther out of Hibbing, Wickman persuaded Orville S. Caesar, a former auto mechanic who operated a bus line out of Superior, Wisconsin, to join forces with him and Bogan. The three embarked on a steady program of buying up bus lines, integrating them into their existing operation, and at the same time steadily extending their routes in all directions. During this period, the trio called their business the Motor Transit Company, although some of its bus lines operated under more colorful names.

The Greyhound name came from one of the small lines operating in western Michigan. A sketch of a racing greyhound was painted on the side of each bus, and patrons referred to it as "the Greyhound line." The name appealed to Wickman and the others as singularly appropriate, and it was adopted quickly for the entire system. That was in 1926.

As early as 1940, plans were made for a revolutionary new bus, the Scenicruiser, but because of World War II, it was not until 1954 that this forty-foot, double-decker bus with washroom facilities, twin diesels, air suspension, and other comforts appeared on the nation's highways.

Wickman died the year the Scenicruiser appeared, leaving Caesar as president and Bogan as executive vice president of a major corporation now owned by more than sixty thousand stockholders. The company proudly called itself "the world's largest passenger transportation company."

Over the next several years, management decided to market the company to business and pleasure travelers. Ads aimed at drivers of private cars were designed to win them over to Greyhound for intercity travel. "It's such a comfort to take the bus—and leave the driving to us," was the text of a singing jingle used extensively.

Greyhound introduced all-expense tours to attract vacation travelers to events such as the Rose Bowl football game, Mardi Gras, and other festivals. The first land-sea trip to Hawaii via Greyhound and Matson Navigation Company sold out quickly.

The company also began hauling small packages, newspapers, and the like in the roomy baggage compartments under each bus. As a result, the company offers its Greyhound PackageXpress, including pickup and delivery service in hundreds of cities in every state except Alaska and Hawaii.

Greyhound has come a long way since that first trip Carl Wickman made in his Hupmobile. From carrying a few dozen passengers a day in 1912, the Greyhound Corporation has become the largest intercity carrier of passengers in the nation.

# 5

---

# RAILROAD REVIVAL

A YEAR AFTER the Erie Canal opened in 1825, the United States' first railroad began hauling blocks of granite cut from a quarry in Quincy, Massachusetts, to the Neponsit River, where the stone was loaded on boats and floated some ten miles over to Charlestown to be used for constructing the Bunker Hill Monument. A second and similar railroad opened the following year in Pennsylvania to transport anthracite coal. However, it was the Baltimore and Ohio Railroad that was the nation's oldest from the standpoint of offering continuous passenger service starting in 1830.

During the 1830s numerous other railroads were laying primitive rails in various parts of the Atlantic coast states. At first most of them provided shuttle service between two cities or towns; a few served as connecting links to two canals that otherwise could not offer their shippers through-service. The latter part of the 1830s witnessed an epidemic of railroad construction with many of today's major lines tracing their origins back to that time. Although by 1840 only 1,098 miles of track had been laid, the public understood the importance of these pioneering companies and what they portended. Soon one canal after another went out of business, and further major road construction and repair were greatly reduced. Railroads were seen as the answer to all transportation needs.

The railroad fever raced throughout the country until the 1870s, when investors feared there had been too much expansion. The resulting stock market railroad panic of 1873 brought such a crash in stock values that further construction practically halted until the 1880s, when more mileage was added than during any previous decade.

Most of this new track was laid in the West. By this time in the East, two or more companies were competing for passenger and freight traffic between most principal cities. After 1916 additional expansion fell off dramatically, and thereafter many railroad companies were finding it increasingly difficult to make a profit, except during World War II. Not only was there fierce competition, but there was also insufficient traffic on numerous branch lines that were no longer profitable.

From here on the story has been mostly one of railroads losing business to airlines, buses, and trucks, abandoning unprofitable main and branch lines, and merging with other companies in a desperate struggle to survive. Finally, the two premier longtime rival lines New York Central and Pennsylvania merged—and then failed. Ironically, this helped create a new day for railroading because the government stepped in to save the transportation crisis in the East by helping give birth to two new rail systems: Amtrak and Conrail.

## Amtrak

By 1970 more than one hundred of the nation's five hundred passenger railroads had asked the Interstate Commerce Commission for permission to discontinue all service; for twenty years most of these privately owned companies had been operating at a loss and were facing bankruptcy. The automobile, which could now speed over the new interstate highway system as well as other improved roads, provided a less expensive and more flexible form of transportation for many families that had formerly traveled by train. At the same time the growth of airline service and the speed of the jets, which could fly coast to coast in fewer than six hours, contrasted heavily with the three-day train trip, making transcontinental rail service practically obsolete. Although some people still preferred to ride trains or were afraid to fly, there were not enough of them to sustain the rail industry.

In October 1970 Congress established Amtrak, officially known as the National Railroad Passenger Corporation. This was a quasi-public corporation, its board of directors composed of eight officers appointed by the president, three representatives from the railroad industry, and four private investors. These investors were chosen from those who held the company's preferred stock.

Congress intended the company to be a profit-making enterprise and gave it an initial grant of $40 million plus $100 million in federal loan guarantees. By the time Amtrak began operating in 1971, it had eliminated half of the intercity passenger service, keeping only those trains that enjoyed dense traffic. During that first year, trains were running over 180 routes and serving approximately three hundred cities. Amtrak is the only intercity carrier. In addition, there are about twenty regional commuter carriers and numerous excursion rail carriers that operate over short rail lines.

For years Japan and France have led the railroad world with their high-speed passenger trains. The United States has since joined the ranks of high-speed leaders with the introduction of Amtrak's newest service, serving the Northeast corridor, which is the busiest railroad in North America, with more than seventeen hundred trains operating over some portion of the Washington–Boston route each day.

### Amtrak's Acela Express Service

Imagine speeding from New York to Washington on the Acela Express Service. Your scheduled running time is a remarkable two hours and forty-five minutes. At-seat electrical outlets for your laptop or DVD player allow you to work or enjoy a movie as you travel in comfort at speeds of 150 miles per hour. Adjustable lighting and large tray tables make it easy to read or to enjoy a meal or snack from the café car.

If you have reserved a first-class seat, you can expect complimentary meals, beverages, and a newspaper, as well as access to the ClubAcela lounge cars. The Acela Express also provides designated quiet cars, and at-seat attendant service is available on selected trains.

Those prophets of doom who say that railroading is obsolete should ride one of these fine trains or some of the other Amtrak lines. They will agree that railroads are not only here to stay but could have an exciting future.

Unfortunately, America's total rail mileage has shrunk considerably over the past fifty years as many unprofitable branches and even main lines were abandoned. As railroad companies merged or went out of business, most of the once luxurious passenger services disappeared. Suburban commuter services, which are operated for the most part by independent authorities created by the state or local government, can continue because of state government subsidies.

# Conrail

Passenger service, however, was not the only part of the railroad industry that needed rescuing. In the years leading to 1973, the freight railroad system of the United States was collapsing. Even after the government-funded Amtrak took over intercity passenger service in 1971, railroad companies continued to lose money. In 1973 Congress introduced a bill to nationalize the bankrupt railroads. On January 2, 1974, President Richard Nixon signed into law the Regional Rail Reorganization Act of 1973. The new law, called the 3R Act, provided interim funding to the bankrupt railroads and defined a new Consolidated Rail Corporation (Conrail).

Conrail was incorporated in 1974, and operations began in April 1976. Authorities hoped that if the service were improved through increased capital investment, the economic basis of the railroad would also be improved. Although Conrail's government-funded rebuilding of the heavily run-down railroad infrastructure and rolling stock it inherited from its six bankrupt predecessors succeeded in improving the physical condition of tracks, locomotives, and freight cars, the fundamental economic regulatory issues remained, and the company continued to post losses of as much as $1 million a day.

Recognizing the need for more regulatory freedoms to address the economic issues, Conrail management lobbied for what became the Staggers Act of 1980, which significantly loosened the Interstate Commerce Commission's economic control of the rail industry. This allowed Conrail and other carriers to become profitable and strengthen their finances by increasing rates and abandoning unprofitable lines, and Conrail began turning a profit by 1981.

Although Conrail inherited and initially operated the commuter rail operations of its predecessors, the Northeast Rail Service Act of 1983 relieved the company of its requirement to provide commuter service in the Northeast corridor, further improving its finances. Commuter services were transferred to state or metropolitan transportation authorities.

Today Conrail operates as a terminal and switching agent for its owners, CSX Transportation and Norfolk Southern. It provides rail service for many local rail freight customers in Detroit, New Jersey, and Philadelphia. Customers located along Conrail's lines in these areas have access to the nation's rail network through either of the two parent companies.

## Canadian Rail

Canada's first railway, the Champlain and St. Lawrence Railroad, began operating from Laprairie, Quebec, to St. Johns (which is now St. Jean), Quebec, in July 1836. In November 1852 the Grand Trunk Railway received its charter, and six months later the first train in Ontario ran between Toronto and Aurora. The next two years saw the opening of the Great Western Railway and the Bytown and Prescott Railway. In June 1872 the Grand Trunk acquired the Champlain and St. Lawrence Railroad, and the Intercolonial Railway was completed in 1876.

The next four decades saw the opening of several new railroads and bridges, the first use of the telephone to dispatch trains, and the introduction of the longest passenger train in the country, among many other achievements on the rails.

Today there are three major rail systems operating in Canada: Canada National Railway, Canadian Pacific Railway, and VIA Rail

Canada. Read the following descriptions of each to see whether they might be right for you.

## Canada National Railway

On June 6, 1919, the Canadian National Railway Company (CN) was created. In 1923 the company took final form with the addition of Grand Trunk Railway. Two years later its diesel-electric car No. 15820 set a world record by traveling from Montreal to Vancouver in sixty-eight and a half hours. In August 1929 CN put the first road diesel-electric passenger locomotive in service between Montreal and Toronto.

The 1930s and 1940s saw many advancements, including the first two-way train phone service and the introduction of diesel-electric locomotives into freight service between Montreal and Toronto. In the next two decades, CN inaugurated the Super Continental passenger service Montreal–Toronto–Vancouver and ran the last of its steam-operated locomotives.

Today Canada National Railway is the nation's primary mover of products such as coal, fertilizer, automobiles, forest products, grain, metals and minerals, and petroleum and chemicals. The main categories of employment that it offers are engineering, mechanical, operations (of yards, terminals, and so forth), and sales and customer service.

The network operations function of CN is a vast section that covers running the trains. Employees work in network transportation, mechanical/engineering, and support functions, including supply management, CN police, environment, and safety.

The function of the sales and marketing division is to manage and market competitive transportation and distribution services to

CN customers. Employees in this area are responsible for developing new customers, promoting the company to current customers, and maximizing CN's participation in market economics. Typical positions in this division are account managers, market managers, and market analysts.

The corporate divisions of CN include finance and strategic planning, human resources, public affairs, legal services, and information technology. Among these divisions, the company employees staff such positions as accountants, human resources specialists, attorneys, programmers, and help-desk analysts.

You can find extensive information about Canada National Railway at www.cn.ca.

## Canadian Pacific Railway

The Canadian Pacific Railway (CPR) provides freight transportation services over a fourteen-thousand-mile network in Canada and the United States. CPR ships such materials as grain, coal, and lumber as well as cars, agricultural equipment, food, and furniture.

Canadian Pacific Railway was founded in 1881 to link Canada's populated centers with the relatively unpopulated West. This incredible engineering feat was completed six years ahead of schedule, on November 7, 1885, when the last spike was driven at Craigellachie, British Columbia. By 1889 the railway extended from coast to coast, and the enterprise had expanded to include a wide range of related and unrelated businesses.

CPR was involved in land settlement and land sales as early as September 1881. The company also erected telegraph lines alongside the main transcontinental line, transmitting its first commercial telegram in 1882. During that year CPR also entered the express shipment business, with the acquisition of the Dominion Express Company. CPR started building some of its own steam locomotives as early as 1883 and would later build its own passenger cars, making it second on the continent only to the Pullman Company of Chicago, Illinois.

CPR had steamships on the Great Lakes in 1883 and chartered ships on the Pacific Ocean in 1886, while launching its own Pacific fleet in 1891. CPR got into paddle wheelers in British Columbia's interior in 1893, on British Columbia's coast in 1901, and on the Atlantic Ocean in 1903. The company was also involved in the hotel and tourist trade as early as 1886, after William Cornelius Van Horne, who was its vice president at the time, suggested setting up a national park system in the Canadian Rockies.

CPR even discovered natural gas on the prairies, although quite by accident. In 1886, while digging a well to get water for its steam locomotives, CPR crews stumbled across natural gas in what is now Alderson, Alberta. The railway would later use the natural gas to heat and power the station and ancillary buildings.

Throughout its history, CPR became involved in many other ventures, including animal husbandry, bus transportation, containers and pallets, forestry, foundries, immigration and colonization, insurance, irrigation, manufacturing, milling and foodstuffs, mines and minerals, newsreels, oil, pulp and paper, radio broadcasts, stockyards, supply farms, trucking, waste management, even bottled spring water. In 1942 CPR even took to the skies, amalgamating ten Northern bush plane companies into Canadian Pacific Airlines.

Today CPR is based in Calgary, Alberta, and it employs more than fifteen thousand people throughout the country. Its fourteen-thousand-mile network extends from the Port of Vancouver in Canada's west to the Port of Montreal in Canada's east, and to the

U.S. industrial centers of Chicago; Newark; Philadelphia; Washington, DC; New York City; and Buffalo.

The company offers educational opportunities for those interested in a rail transportation career: a new graduate program, open to new graduates of postsecondary institutions; a summer student program, for those currently enrolled in secondary or postsecondary institutions; and a co-op education program, again for postsecondary students. In addition, CPR offers $1,000 scholarships to women pursuing careers as railway conductors.

It is also possible to complete a college railway-training program through one of several postsecondary institutions that offer the required technical training for such positions as conductor, rail traffic controller, and signals and communications worker, among others. In Canada, programs are offered by Southern Alberta Institute of Technology (Calgary), Northern Alberta Institute of Technology (Stettler), British Columbia Institute of Technology (Vancouver), George Brown College (Toronto), College Gerald-Godin (Montreal), and Institute of Railway Technology (Ottawa). In the United States, programs are offered by Johnson County Community College (Kansas City, Missouri) and Dakota County Technical College (Rosemount, Minnesota).

For complete information on the Canadian Pacific Railway, visit www8.cpr.ca.

## VIA Rail Canada

VIA Rail Canada is an independent corporation established in 1976 as a division of Canada National Railway. VIA operates trains in all regions of Canada over a network spanning the country from the Atlantic to the Pacific and from the Great Lakes to Hudson Bay.

Commuter trains run over fourteen thousand kilometers of track, serving more than 450 communities. Nearly four million passengers use VIA each year. The company employs more than three thousand staff to maintain its operations as:

- Service attendants
- Station attendants
- Counter sales agents
- Telephone sales agents
- Electricians
- Heavy-duty mechanics and heavy-duty mechanics-welders
- Heavy-duty mechanics, specialists
- General workers

For detailed information about VIA and its many career possibilities, visit www.viarail.ca.

## Commuter Railroads

Although it is true that the early trolleys made it possible for city dwellers to move out to less-congested areas, later the railroads greatly extended the distance people could conveniently travel to their homes from metropolitan centers. Today most large cities offer good commuter rail service, usually operated by metropolitan or regional authorities. In some cases the railroads contract to run the trains; in others the authority may lease or even purchase the tracks and stations and is responsible for train operation. Because these services are so essential year-round, they offer secure jobs usually with good incomes. Contact the human resources office of the railroad or authority in your city for employment information.

## Major Rail Lines

Over the years, many of the larger freight carriers have prospered in varying degrees. With past and contemplated mergers of large lines, the prospect of fewer but more efficient railroads has been encouraging to many shippers, which are the lifeblood of railroads now that passenger service is operated mostly by Amtrak.

In 1980 the Staggers Rail Act reduced much of the former government red tape and interference with railroad operation, making trains much more competitive with trucks and water carriers. It allowed railroads to sign long-term contracts in return for guaranteed volume, which meant lower rates for the shippers and steady business for the carriers. Railroads could at last change their rates when necessary to meet the competition without waiting months or years for government approval. This change enabled them to attract business from the highways for the first time.

One area where this was especially beneficial was in the so-called *piggyback* business. This term refers to the movement of truck trailers and containers on rail flatcars. Instead of waiting for Interstate Commerce Commission permission to increase or lower rates for this kind of business, railroads can match truck rates and initiate their own price changes daily, if necessary.

Just as some of the large truckers keep close track of their trucks, the railroads are improving their ability to spot freight cars wherever they may be. This is important to shippers who often must know where their goods are and when they will be delivered. More important, of course, is a railroad's ability to deliver the freight on schedule, when promised, and at a cost competitive with other forms of ground transportation.

# Short-Line Railroads

Short-line railroads, run for tourists and/or railroad buffs, operate in various parts of the country. Probably the two best known are the Mount Washington and the Pikes Peak cog railways. These are seasonal operations that employ about two dozen men and women each. Many of the employees are college students interested in learning about the railroad industry and earning money for their education. In addition, there are numerous restored rail lines over which steam or diesel power pulls a wide variety of equipment ranging from antique passenger cars to refurbished commuter coaches.

Most of the miniature roads are staffed by railroad buffs who work for the fun of it, but jobs on such lines provide experience as well as an opportunity to learn whether railroading is for you. If interested, write to your state public utility commission for a list of such railroads and inquire about employment opportunities.

## *The White Pass and Yukon Route*

One fascinating short-line railroad is the White Pass and Yukon Route in Skagway, Alaska. Built in 1898 during the Klondike gold rush, this narrow-gauge railway transported prospectors from Skagway to the summit of the White Pass. This might not seem to be such a tremendous undertaking, until you realize that the White Pass climbs an elevation of 2,865 feet, which the train travels in twenty miles, moving through two tunnels and over amazingly high trestles to reach its destination.

Although construction of the White Pass and Yukon Route was considered impossible, it was nonetheless accomplished in twenty-six months through a combination of British financing, American engineering, and Canadian contracting. Tens of thousands of men and 450 tons of explosives overcame harsh and challenging climate and geography to create the "railway built of gold." The steel cantilever bridge was the tallest of its kind in the world when it was constructed in 1901.

The 110-mile railroad was completed with the driving of the golden spike on July 29, 1900, in Carcross, Yukon, connecting the deepwater port of Skagway to Whitehorse, Yukon, and beyond to northwest Canada and interior Alaska.

The White Pass and Yukon Route became a fully integrated transportation company operating docks, trains, stagecoaches, sleighs, buses, paddle wheelers, trucks, ships, airplanes, hotels, and pipelines. It provided the essential infrastructure servicing the freight and passenger requirements of Yukon's population and mining industry. The company proved to be a successful transportation innovator and pioneered the intermodal (ship-train-truck) movement of containers.

The White Pass and Yukon Route suspended operations in 1982 when Yukon's mining industry collapsed due to low mineral prices. The railway was reopened in 1988 as a seasonal tourism operation and served 37,000 passengers. Today, it is Alaska's most popular shore excursion, carrying more than 431,000 passengers in 2006 during the May to September tourism season, while operating on the first 67.5 miles (Skagway, Alaska, to Carcross, Yukon) of the original 110-mile line.

The company employs seasonal workers in such occupations as tour guide/passenger agent, gift shop clerk, restocker, shuttle driver, ticket agent, and barista. You can get complete information about the railroad by visiting its website at www.wpyr.com.

# Job Descriptions

Many look with enthusiasm at the career possibilities that exist elsewhere in railroad companies. Let's see what employment opportunities there are in the three principal divisions of a railroad.

## *Administrative*

Railroads are no different from other industries that require a wide variety of clerical and other administrative personnel. Accordingly, you will find clerks and secretaries working in various specialized positions. Railroads also employ administrative staff in the advertising, computer, labor relations, legal, personnel, public relations, purchasing, and sales departments. Other specialists are scattered throughout the entire organization.

## *Maintenance*

Making certain that engines, freight and passenger cars, as well as tracks, signals, and communications equipment are in perfect working order is the responsibility of this division. Because trains operate around the clock, continuous attention must be paid to every part of the operation.

One of the specialized jobs in this division is that of car repairer, who may be assigned to check rolling stock as it comes into a terminal or work in the repair shop performing necessary maintenance or major overhauls. Mechanics are assigned to diesel engines and other motorized equipment, while electricians repair and service electrical equipment in locomotives and cars. They also work on air conditioners and other electrical apparatuses. Workers with a variety of skills make repairs on motors as well as engine and car frames; replace parts such as fuel lines, air hoses, valves, and wheels; or rebuild engine transmissions.

Out on the right-of-way, gangs of workers replace rails and ties and tamp down ballast to keep tracks in top condition. Others repair and paint bridges, clean culverts, and dig ditches alongside the roadbed. Much of this work is now performed by intricate machinery, which decreases the need for the large section gangs. However, some employees are required to operate the machines.

Communications are important to safe operations. Trained maintenance workers service the all-important signal system. They also repair the telephone, radio, and microwave systems. Radio is used so that engineers can talk with their conductors a mile away in the caboose and personnel can communicate with each other in the yards and between stations.

## Transportation

Engineers, brake operators, and conductors run the engines. In the days of the coal-fired steam engines, a fireman was an important member of the engine crew. However, with the advent of diesels, the services of a fireman were eliminated.

Engineers operate locomotives in passenger, freight, or yard service. Passenger trains run on tight schedules, and it is the engineer's job to reach each station on time. If the train is delayed by red signals or for other reasons, he or she tries to make up for lost time without sacrificing safety.

Freight engineers pilot freight trains, which may be either fast freights operating on set schedules or local freights that pick up and drop cars at way stations. They, too, operate according to a schedule but are not necessarily held to it because the number of cars to be switched varies from day to day.

Yard engineers who run the switching engines make up trains by sorting out cars and pulling or pushing them to the tracks where they will be coupled to form new trains.

Brake operators ride on the trains: one rides in the caboose with the conductor, and the other rides up front in the cab with the engineer. In the old days, before the air brake was invented, brakemen were exactly what their name implies. They operated the hand brakes on freight and passenger cars on a signal from the engineer. It was dangerous work, running back and forth on top of swaying freight cars in icy or snowy weather. It is still dangerous because when a freight train approaches a siding to pick up or drop off cars, the brake operator jumps off the engine and runs ahead to set the switches.

The brake operator also couples and uncouples cars at terminals, stations, and sidings. In the yards, he or she couples and uncouples cars and throws switches. The brake operator often climbs up a car to ride with it and control its speed with the hand brake as it rolls down an incline to be joined with a series of cars that are being made into a train.

Brake operators on passenger trains have it much easier. They watch over the operation of the cars and their equipment. They also use flags and flares to protect the train from a rear-end collision whenever the train is forced to make an unscheduled stop.

Conductors are in charge of all trains: passenger, freight, or yard. Yard conductors supervise the workers and also make up trains.

## Working Conditions

Many rail transportation employees work nights, weekends, and holidays, because trains operate twenty-four hours a day, seven days a week. Many work more than a forty-hour workweek. Seniority usually dictates who receives the more desirable shifts.

Many freight trains are dispatched according to the needs of customers; as a result, train crews have irregular schedules. Workers often place their names on a list and wait for their turn to work, with jobs generally assigned on short notice and often at odd hours; working weekends is common. Those who work on trains operating between points hundreds of miles apart may spend several nights at a time away from home.

Workers on passenger trains ordinarily have regular and reliable shifts. In addition, they work in more comfortable surroundings than their colleagues on freight trains.

Rail-yard workers spend most of their time outdoors and work regardless of the weather. The work of conductors and engineers on local runs, on which trains stop frequently at stations to pick up and deliver cars, is physically demanding. Climbing up and down and getting off moving cars is strenuous and can be dangerous.

## Job Qualifications and Training

If you'd like to work in railroad transportation, you will probably begin as a yard laborer and work toward the opportunity to train for a job as engineer or conductor. Railroads will require that you have at least a high school diploma or its equivalent. Physical stamina is required for entry-level jobs, and you'll need to have good eyesight, hearing, hand-eye coordination, manual dexterity, and mechanical aptitude.

You will have to pass a physical exam, drug and alcohol screening, and a criminal background check. To operate an engine, federal regulations require the railroad to check your driving record for any evidence of drug or alcohol problems, and you will be subject to random drug and alcohol testing while on duty.

To apply for a job as locomotive engineer, you must be at least twenty-one years old, and experience in other railroad-operating occupations is always a plus. In keeping with federal regulations, you'll have to complete a formal engineer training program, including classroom, simulator, and hands-on instruction in locomotive operation. The instruction is usually administered by the rail company in programs approved by the Federal Railroad Administration. At the end of the training period, you will have to pass a hearing and visual acuity test, a safety conduct background check, a railroad operation knowledge test, and a skills performance test. The company will issue your engineer's license after you pass the examinations. Other conditions and rules may apply to entry-level engineers and usually vary with the employer.

To maintain certification, engineers are monitored by their companies. In addition to this monitoring, they are required to periodically pass an operational rules efficiency test. The test is an unannounced event requiring engineers to take active or responsive action in certain situations, such as maintaining a particular speed through a curve or yard.

Engineers undergo periodic physical examinations and drug and alcohol testing to determine their fitness to operate locomotives. In some cases, those who fail to meet these physical and conduct standards are restricted to yard service; in other instances, they may be disciplined, trained to perform other work, or discharged.

Railroads generally fill conductor jobs from the ranks of experienced rail transportation workers who have passed tests covering signals, timetables, operating rules, and related subjects. Seniority usually is the main factor in determining promotion to conductor.

To be employed as an entry-level conductor, you will have to be at least twenty-one years of age and either be trained by your employer or complete a formal conductor training program through a community college.

As a newly trained engineer or conductor, you'll be placed on the "extra board" until permanent positions become available. In this capacity you will receive assignments only when the railroad needs substitutes for regular workers who are absent because of vacation, illness, or other reasons. Seniority rules may allow workers with greater seniority to select their type of assignment. For example, an engineer may move from an initial, regular assignment in yard service to road service.

For brake and signal operator jobs, railroad firms will train applicants either in a company program or at an outside training facility. Typical training programs combine classroom and on-site training and last between four and six weeks for signal operators and between ten and eighteen weeks for brake operators.

Most subway and transit systems prefer applicants for subway and streetcar operator jobs to possess at least a high school education. Because most transit systems also operate buses, you'll probably start as a bus driver. For this job, you must be in good health, have good communication skills, and be able to make quick, responsible judgments. New operators generally complete training programs that last anywhere from a few weeks to six months. At the end of the period of classroom and on-the-job training, you will usually be required to pass qualifying examinations. These examinations cover the operating system, troubleshooting, and evacuation and emergency procedures on the bus. Some operators with sufficient seniority can advance to station manager or another supervisory position.

A commercial driver's license might be required for yard occupations because these workers often operate trucks and other heavy vehicles.

## Earnings

Most railroad workers are paid according to miles traveled or hours worked, whichever leads to higher earnings. Full-time employees have steadier work, more regular hours, increased opportunities for overtime work, and higher earnings than do those assigned to the extra board.

Median hourly earnings of rail transportation occupations were relatively high in 2004, as indicated here:

| | |
|---|---|
| Locomotive engineers | $24.30 |
| Subway and streetcar operators | $23.70 |
| Railroad conductors and yardmasters | $22.28 |
| Railroad brake, signal, and switch operators | $21.46 |

Rail transportation workers in Canada had average hourly earnings in 2004 as shown:

| | |
|---|---|
| Transportation (scheduling, dispatching, and operating trains) | $25.20 |
| Track maintenance | $25.10 |
| Equipment maintenance | $26.70 |
| Administrative services | $34.80 |

Eight out of ten railroad transportation workers are members of unions. Many different railroad unions represent various crafts on the railroads. Most railroad engineers are members of the Brotherhood of Locomotive Engineers and Trainmen, while most other railroad transportation workers are members of the United Transportation Union. Many subway operators are members of the Amalgamated Transit Union, while others belong to the Transport Workers Union of North America.

## Employment Outlook

Railroads employ about 82 percent of all railroad workers, with the balance working for local transit companies and manufacturing and mining companies that operate their own railroad equipment. According to estimated figures, employment statistics in 2004 were as follows: locomotive engineers, 40,000; railroad conductors and yardmasters, 38,000; railroad brake, signal, and switch operators, 17,000; subway and streetcar operators, 9,200; and all other rail transportation workers, 8,100.

Although employment in most railroad occupations is expected to decline through the year 2014, opportunities are expected to be good for qualified applicants, due mainly to the large number of workers expected to retire or leave the industry.

Opportunities are expected to be better for long-distance train crews than for yard jobs, which generally require little education beyond high school and don't require as much travel. Employment of streetcar and subway operators should grow between 9 and 17 percent, due to increased demand for light-rail transportation systems around the country.

Demand for railroad freight service is expected to grow as the economy and the intermodal transportation of goods expand. Intermodal systems use trucks to move shippers' sealed trailers or containers to and from terminals and use fuel-efficient trains to transport them over the long distances between terminals. In an effort to compete with other modes of transportation such as trucks, ships, and aircraft, railroads are improving delivery times and on-time service while reducing shipping rates.

Job growth among railroad transportation workers may be adversely affected by innovations such as larger, faster, more fuel-efficient trains and computerized classification yards that make it possible to move freight more efficiently. Computers help to keep track of freight cars, match empty cars with the closest loads, and dispatch and control trains. Computer-assisted devices alert engineers to any malfunctions, and work rules now allow trains to operate with two-person crews instead of the traditional three- to five-person crews.

# 6

# Our Love Affair
# with Automobiles

ALTHOUGH IT IS true that the airplane changed much of the world
by making it possible to travel and ship goods between cities and
nations in a matter of hours, it was the mass production of automobiles that within a few decades brought about the greatest
changes in our lifestyles, economy, and environment.

We can be certain that back in 1600 when Dutchman Simon
Steven built his "sailing chariot"—a wagon propelled by wind—he
was only trying to devise a vehicle that would operate without
horsepower, not revolutionize how the world would eventually
travel. Obviously, when the wind died down, the vehicle was use-
less, which is why in 1796 Nicolas Cugnot used steam to make the
first self-propelled vehicle. Frightened by similar developments in
England, Parliament passed various laws restricting these steam-

powered vehicles. Finally it adopted the Red Flag Act of 1865, which required a rider on horseback to carry a red flag ahead of each such vehicle (sort of like the escort vehicles you see today announcing that an oversized load follows).

At the beginning of the nineteenth century, Oliver Evans, an American, achieved the same success using steam, but it was not until 1883 that the Duryea brothers used their gas-fired engine to run a carriage through the muddy streets of Springfield, Massachusetts. Two years later a Rochester, New York, lawyer, George B. Selden, patented his internal combustion engine, which was copied by numerous would-be auto inventors, including Henry Ford of Detroit. In 1908 Ford brought out his Model T and in 1913 started mass producing his black "Tin Lizzies." By 1927, when Ford discontinued the Model T for a more modern Model A, the company had produced fifteen million cars. As the Model A's came off the assembly lines, most of the independent manufacturers gradually disappeared, and by 1949 Chrysler, Ford, and General Motors were producing 85 percent of all American-made cars.

We have previously pointed out that the United States had to build a vast network of roads and highways to accommodate the ever-growing number of cars and trucks. A more serious problem gradually developed as the number of gasoline-driven vehicles increased. Gasoline fumes were contributing to alarming environmental problems. In many cities where temperature inversion trapped smog for several days, half of the pollutants were attributed to gasoline fumes. At the same time it was suspected that these fumes were also contributing to the greenhouse effect, or heat buildup in the earth's atmosphere, and some states began to pass laws requiring that a minimum percentage of all cars sold by a manufacturer in those states be powered by electricity.

In 1997 Toyota introduced its Prius, the first production hybrid vehicle, which can operate on gasoline or electricity. By 2007 most major auto manufacturers offered hybrids, ranging from compact cars to sport utility vehicles to full-size pick-up trucks. One of the advantages of hybrid-electric vehicles (HEVs) is that unlike all-electric vehicles, the HEVs now being offered do not need to be plugged into an external source of electricity to be recharged; conventional gasoline and a regenerative braking system provide all the energy the vehicle needs.

## Importance of the Automobile Industry

This book discusses transportation, not manufacturing of the various types of machines or vehicles that carry passengers and cargo. Thus we have not covered shipbuilding or the manufacture of buses, light rail cars, trolleys, airplanes, or railroad equipment. However, we are making an exception in the case of automobiles and light trucks because auto manufacturing plants offer many career opportunities and are closely tied to various peripheral service businesses that support the industry once automobiles and trucks leave the factories. In the last decade, light trucks have dominated the light-vehicle assembly line, with pickup trucks, minivans, and sport utility vehicles accounting for over 70 percent of total sales.

Excluding those who work in agriculture, one out of every seven jobs in the United States is related to the manufacture and use of automobiles and light trucks, which gives employment to some twelve million Americans. In the auto sales and service industry, which includes the service station down the street, more than $200 billion change hands each year.

## Automobile Plants

The automobile industry in North America has changed over the last several years. While once there were three principal "Detroit" manufacturers (Chrysler, Ford, and General Motors), today mergers and the growing number of foreign operations in the United States and Canada have altered the picture. Ford and General Motors still have Detroit-based operations. In addition, Toyota, Honda, and Subaru are among the foreign companies that maintain operations plants in the United States and Canada.

At last count, about ninety-four establishments manufactured motor vehicles and parts; these ranged from small parts plants with only a few workers to huge assembly plants that employ thousands.

The North American motor vehicle and parts manufacturing industry has become increasingly integrated into the international economy. In fact, many "domestic" vehicles are produced using the components, manufacturing plants, and distribution methods of other nations around the world, as U.S. and foreign auto manufacturers benefit from strategic alliances in the design, production, and distribution of vehicles and parts. Collaboration in manufacturing practices has dramatically increased productivity and improved efficiency. These cooperative practices also have resulted in manufacturers from the United States, Europe, and the Pacific Rim working closely with parts suppliers and locating production plants in the countries in which they plan to sell their vehicles, to reduce distribution time and costs. Foreign motor vehicle and parts makers with production sites in the United States are known as *domestic internationals* and account for a growing share of U.S. production and employment.

Globalization of the industry has also boosted competition among U.S. manufacturers, prompting innovations in product design and in the manufacturing process. Manufacturers have rapidly designed and produced new models aimed at niches in the market. Firms must be fast and flexible in implementing new production techniques, such as replacing traditional assembly lines with modern systems using computers, robots, and interchangeable platforms. Plants designed for production flexibility put resources in the right place at the right time, allowing manufacturers to shift to new models quickly and efficiently.

## Occupations in the Industry

Manufacturing motor vehicles requires a large number of employees working in a variety of positions.

Production workers account for about 64 percent of motor vehicle and parts manufacturing jobs. Assemblers and fabricators and metal workers and plastic workers put together various parts to form subassemblies and then put the subassemblies together to build a complete vehicle. Most assemblers are team assemblers, who may work on a variety of tasks as needed. Some may perform other routine tasks such as mounting and inflating tires, adjusting brakes, and adding gas, oil, brake fluid, and coolant. Metal parts are welded, plastic and glass parts are molded and cut, seat cushions are sewn, and many parts are painted.

Because many of the manufacturing processes are highly automated, robots, computers, and programmable devices are an integral part of motor vehicle manufacturing. Although robotics perform most of the welding, workers who weld, solder, and braze still are needed for some tasks and for maintenance and repair duties. Machinists produce precision metal parts that are made in numbers too small to produce with automated machinery. Tool and die makers produce tools, dies, and special guiding and holding devices used in machines. Computer-controlled machine tool operators use computer-controlled machines or robots programmed to manufacture parts of different dimensions automatically.

Workers in other production occupations run various machines that produce an array of motor vehicle bodies and parts. They set up and operate machines and make adjustments according to their instructions. In computer-controlled systems, they monitor the computers that run the machine processes and may have little interaction with the machinery or materials. Some workers specialize in one type of machine; others operate more than one type.

Grinding and polishing workers use hand tools or hand-held power tools to sand and polish metal surfaces, and painters paint surfaces of motor vehicles. Sewing machine operators sew together pieces of material to form seat covers and other parts.

Throughout the manufacturing process, inspectors, testers, sorters, samplers, and weighers ensure that the vehicles and parts meet quality standards. They inspect raw materials, check parts for defects, check the uniformity of subassemblies, and test-drive vehicles. Helpers clean work areas and equipment.

The movement of materials and finished products is essential to keeping the plant running smoothly. Industrial truck and tractor operators carry components, equipment, and other materials from factory warehouse and outdoor storage areas to assembly areas. Truck drivers carry raw materials to plants, components and materials between plants, and finished motor vehicles to dealerships for sale to consumers. Laborers and hand freight, stock, and material movers manually move materials to and from storage areas, loading docks, delivery vehicles, and containers. Machine feeders and offbearers feed materials into, or remove materials from, machines or equipment on the assembly line, and hand packers and packagers manually package or wrap materials.

Workers in construction, installation, maintenance, and repair occupations set up, maintain, and repair all the equipment. Electricians service complex electrical equipment. Industrial machinery mechanics and machinery maintenance workers maintain machinery and equipment to prevent costly breakdowns and, when necessary, perform repairs. Millwrights install and move machinery and heavy equipment according to the factory's layout plans. Automotive service technicians and mechanics fix bodies, engines, and other parts of motor vehicles, industrial trucks, and other mobile heavy equipment.

You should keep in mind that the positions just described are those that take place during vehicle assembly. Before a motor vehicle can be built, however, commercial and industrial designers; mechanical, electrical, and industrial engineers; computer systems analysts; and production managers and supervisors all contribute to the design of each model built.

## Qualifications and Training

Since technological advances and the continuing need to cut costs have become a standard part of the automotive industry, manufacturers emphasize continuing education and cross-train many workers to do more than one job. Therefore, while there used to be many opportunities for unskilled workers in the industry, standards for new employees are now higher than in the past.

You will most likely need at least a high school diploma as the number of unskilled jobs declines, and most manufacturers administer lengthy examinations when hiring assemblers. You'll need manual dexterity for many production jobs, but employers also look for employees with good communication and math skills, as well as an aptitude for computers, problem solving, and critical thinking. Because many plants now emphasize the team approach, employees interact more with coworkers and supervisors to determine the best way to get the job done. In this setting, you will be expected to work with a minimum of supervision and to be responsible for ensuring that the work conforms to guidelines.

Opportunities for training and advancement vary considerably by occupation, plant size, and sector. Training programs in larger auto and light-truck assembly plants usually are more extensive than those in smaller parts, truck-trailer, and motor-home factories. Production workers receive most of their training on the job or through more formal apprenticeship programs. Training normally takes from a few days to several months and may combine classroom with on-the-job training under the guidance of more experienced workers. Attaining the highest level of skill in some production jobs requires several years. Training often includes courses in health and safety, teamwork, and quality control. With advanced training and experience, production workers can advance to inspector or to more skilled production, craft, operator, or repair jobs.

Skilled production workers, such as tool and die makers, millwrights, machinists, pipe fitters, and electricians, normally are hired on the basis of previous experience and, in some cases, a competitive examination. Alternatively, the company may train inexperienced workers in apprenticeship programs that last up to five years and combine on-the-job training with classroom instruction. Typical courses include mechanical drawing, tool designing and programming, blueprint reading, shop mathematics, hydraulics, and electronics. Training also includes courses on health and safety, teamwork, quality control, computers, and diagnostic equipment. With training and experience, workers who excel can advance to become supervisors or managers.

Manufacturers provide formal training opportunities to all workers, regardless of educational background, and may pay tuition for workers who enroll in colleges, trade schools, or technical institutes. Workers sometimes can get college credit for training received on the job. Subjects of company training courses range from communication skills to computer science. Formal educational opportunities at postsecondary institutions range from courses in English, basic mathematics, electronics, and computer programming languages to work-study programs leading to associate, bachelor's, and graduate degrees in engineering and technician specialties, management, and other fields.

## Earnings

Average weekly earnings of production or nonsupervisory workers in the motor vehicle and parts manufacturing industry are relatively high. At $1,217 per week, earnings of production workers in establishments that manufacture complete motor vehicles were among the highest in the nation in 2004. Workers in establishments that make motor vehicle parts averaged $872 weekly, and those in motor vehicle body and trailer manufacturing earned $690 per week, compared with $659 for workers in all manufacturing industries.

Employees are paid on an hourly basis, and earnings generally increase during overtime or special shifts. Workers generally are paid one and a half times their normal wage rate for working more than eight hours a day or more than forty hours a week or for working on Saturdays. They may receive double their normal wage rate for working on Sundays and holidays. The largest manufacturers and suppliers often offer other benefits, including paid vacations and holidays; life, accident, and health insurance; education allowances; nonwage cash payment plans, such as performance and profit-sharing bonuses; and pension plans. Some laid-off workers in the motor vehicle and parts manufacturing industry have access to supplemental unemployment benefits, which can provide them with nearly full pay and benefits for up to several years, depending on the worker's seniority.

About three out of ten workers in motor vehicle and parts production are union members or are covered by union contracts, more than double the proportion of workers in all manufacturing industries and all workers in the private sector. Workers in motor vehicle production are more likely to be members of unions than are workers in parts production. The primary union in the industry is the United Auto Workers (UAW). Nearly all production workers in motor vehicle assembly plants, and most of those in motor vehicle parts plants, are covered by collective bargaining agreements negotiated by the UAW. Other unions, including the International Association of Machinists and Aerospace Workers of America, the United Steelworkers of America, and the International Brotherhood of Electrical Workers, cover certain plant locations or specified trades in the industry.

## Employment Outlook

Overall wage and salary employment in the motor vehicle and parts manufacturing industry is expected to increase by 6 percent through 2014, compared with 14 percent for all industries combined. Although employment is expected to grow very slowly, firms manufacturing motor vehicle parts, bodies, and trailers are expected to add more jobs. Employment is expected to increase by only 2 percent in motor vehicle manufacturing, with increases of 6 percent in motor vehicle parts manufacturing and 8 percent in motor vehicle body and trailer manufacturing.

Growth in firms that manufacture motor vehicle parts, bodies, and trailers will generate many job openings, as will the departure of workers who retire or transfer to jobs in other industries. However, not all of the motor vehicle manufacturing workers who leave the industry will be replaced, and many of the new workers will be hired for occupations different from those vacated by departing employees.

The demand for motor vehicles and parts should enhance employment, but jobs will be lost due to productivity increases. The growing international and domestic competition has increased cost pressures on manufacturers, who have sought to improve productivity and quality with high-technology production techniques including computer-assisted design, production, and testing. Increasing productivity should meet much of the demand created by the increasing output of the motor vehicle and parts manufacturing industry, resulting in slow job growth. In addition, the industry is increasingly turning to contract employees in an effort to reduce costs. Contract workers are less costly to hire and lay off than are permanent employees; contract jobs also serve as a screening tool for candidates for permanent jobs that are more complex and require more skills.

Employment is highly sensitive to cyclical swings in the economy. During periods of economic prosperity, consumers are more willing and able to purchase expensive goods such as motor vehicles, which may require large down payments and extended loan payments. During recessions, however, consumers are more likely to delay such purchases. Motor vehicle manufacturers respond to these changes in demand by hiring or laying off workers.

## Automobile-Related Careers

Once a vehicle comes off the assembly line, it may be available for a number of other automobile-related careers.

### Taxicab Drivers

In 1926 Sol Baron opened the Cab Operating Company in Brooklyn, New York. He bought one car and hired a driver to operate it. Sol was a mechanic and made certain the cab was always in good running order. Once he'd purchased more cars, Sol's wife became the dispatcher, telling the drivers where to go, checking their reports, and making certain they did not cheat the company. On the company's seventy-fifth anniversary in 2001, Cab Operating, one of the nineteen remaining fleets in New York City, owned eighty cars and enjoyed a good reputation with the Taxi and Limousine Commission, which regulates taxicabs in that metropolis.

In a large city like New York, taxi regulation is strict. The number of cabs that cruise the streets, free to pick up fares on demand, is limited; another group of cabs may respond only to telephone calls. But in Rumney, New Hampshire, a tiny town, anyone who has a car, a chauffeur's license, and proper insurance can operate a taxi service.

Work hours of taxi drivers and chauffeurs vary greatly. Some jobs offer full-time or part-time employment with work hours that can change from day to day or remain the same every day. It is often necessary for drivers to report to work on short notice.

Full-time taxi drivers usually work one shift a day, which may last from eight to twelve hours. Part-time drivers may work half a shift each day or work a full shift once or twice a week. Drivers may work shifts at all times of the day and night because most taxi companies offer services twenty-four hours a day. Early morning and late night shifts are not uncommon. Drivers work long hours during holidays, weekends, and other special times when demand for their services may be heavier. Independent drivers, however, often set their own hours and schedules.

Driving a taxi can be an uncertain occupation. If you are in a large city, you need an encyclopedic knowledge of its streets and must also know where to cruise or wait for the best fares. If you live in a smaller city or town, you probably will receive your jobs at the taxi office, which takes all taxi requests by phone. In this case, you must sit and wait for a call because there would be no point cruising to find business.

In some cities the job can be hazardous, especially if you must drive into high-crime areas. No two days will ever be alike. Your income will depend on tips, and in addition you may receive between 40 and 50 percent of the fares you collect. It can be a long day's work, you may or may not be busy, and you could find it tiring to sit behind the wheel all that time. On the other hand, many drivers would not trade their jobs because they enjoy the freedom and the element of surprise such occupations entail. Of the 188,000 drivers who held jobs in 2004, about 27 percent were self-employed.

Although a high school diploma may not be necessary to land a job as a taxi driver, you should have taken a driver education course and have a chauffeur's license. In some cities you may need a permit to drive as well. Check with your motor vehicle office for the requirements in your area and inquire about job prospects at the office of each taxi company.

## Limousine Drivers

You may live in an area where there is a demand for chauffeurs. Unlike taxi drivers who are at the beck and call of the public, limousine chauffeurs or drivers work for one employer: a business, which has a car to drive officers and other employees to distant points; government agencies, which must provide transportation for some of their top administrators; resorts; private schools; car rental agencies, which might need you to drive cars from the rental office to the garage and back; and livery companies, which rent chauffeur-driven limousines to wealthy customers and for special occasions such as weddings.

Some chauffeurs may be hired by people who prefer to be driven in their own cars. Other chauffeurs own their own cars, which they drive for customers who have special transportation needs.

Chauffeurs must have a chauffeur's license. They usually wear a uniform or a dark business suit and should be well mannered, attentive, and ready to render various small services and courtesies to their employers.

Earnings of taxi drivers and chauffeurs vary greatly, depending on factors such as the number of hours worked, regulatory conditions, customers' tips, and geographic location. Median hourly earnings of salaried taxi drivers and chauffeurs, including tips, were $9.41; most earned between $7.61 and $11.94 an hour.

## Paratransit Drivers

Some drivers transport individuals with special needs, such as those with disabilities and the elderly. These drivers, known as *paratransit drivers*, operate specially equipped vehicles designed to accommodate a variety of needs in nonemergency situations. Although special certification is not necessary, some additional training on the equipment and passenger needs may be required.

## *Service Station Employees*

Although the majority of gasoline stations today are self-service, even at those stations where customers fill their own tanks there must be attendants to take the money and make certain the pumps are operating satisfactorily. There are still some service stations where attendants operate the pumps, clean the windshields, and check the oil.

Such service stations also employ mechanics to repair and service cars. If a mechanic's job is interesting to you, you might start working at the gas pumps and then ask to be given assignments in the shop repairing flat tires, changing oil, lubricating, or checking brake linings. If you have the ability, you might become a junior mechanic working under an experienced person. Should the station have a tow truck, you might be responsible for answering emergency calls and bringing disabled vehicles to the station.

Many high schools offer automotive repair courses as do vocational or technical schools. With this training you will be far more useful to the service station owner than the applicant who has no skills. Good mechanics are usually in demand, the work is varied and interesting, and the pay is good.

Future employment prospects for automotive body repairers, who fix damaged cars and straighten bent bodies, are good. Every day thousands of motor vehicles are involved in traffic accidents, and most can be repaired to function and look like new. As the population increases and more cars are on the road, the need for expert repairers will increase.

## Car Rental Agencies

Car rental companies are found at airports, in downtown areas of cities, and in some suburbs and many small towns. At the reservation counters, agents take reservations by phone or in person. These clerks fill out the necessary forms, telephone the garage for vehicles, and make certain that each customer understands the terms of the rental agreement. Drivers bring the cars from the garage and take them back when they are returned. At the garage, mechanics keep the cars in top running order, while cleaners make certain they are immaculate inside and out.

A high school diploma will qualify you for simple clerical positions that may be available. Qualifications for mechanics were mentioned in the previous section, but openings for cleaners or other unskilled labor would be available on a first-come basis regardless of educational attainments.

## Parking Attendants

In most cities and large towns, parking lots are a necessity for storing the automobiles that are driven into the crowded business districts. Although it is estimated that 90 percent of the parking lots and garages have automatic toll collectors, there are many that hire attendants to park cars. In some large parking garages, attendants drive the cars up ramps or onto elevators, which lift them to whatever floor has parking space available.

## Driving Instructors

Public schools and private driving schools employ driving instructors who teach their students while driving in dual-control training cars.

Requirements for this job vary from state to state, but you should be a high school graduate, be at least twenty-one years old, have a driver's license, and have a good driving record. Inquire at your local board of education and the offices of commercial driving schools regarding possible openings.

For further information contact the Taxicab, Limousine, and Paratransit Association at www.tlpa.org or the American Driver and Traffic Safety Education Association at www.adtsea.iup.edu.

# 7

# FLYING: AN
# UP-AND-DOWN BUSINESS

OVER THE LAST two thousand years, humans have dreamed of somehow flying through the air. Leonardo da Vinci (1452–1519) was the first to accurately record his studies of this challenge, basing his work an observations of bats, birds, and other flying creatures. It was balloons—lighter-than-air vehicles filled with buoyant gas—that opened the door to flight. The first successful ascent took place in France in 1783, followed by many short trips throughout Europe. However, free-flying balloons were not the answer because they drifted according to the direction and speed of air currents and could not be steered with any reliability. The problem was solved in 1890 when a German, Count Ferdinand von Zeppelin, devised a stronger balloon and invented the first successful motor-driven airship. This led to the development of huge, highly flammable, hydrogen-filled balloons to which passenger cabins and engines were attached.

In the 1920s and 1930s large *zeppelins* (airships named for the count) were offering luxurious regularly scheduled service in Europe and on flights to and from North and South America. On one such trip to Lakehurst, New Jersey, the newly built *Hindenburg* caught fire at its mooring post, and the huge loss of life ended further interest in this type of travel.

Even before powered airships were perfected, many inventors were working on different types of heavier-than-air flying machines. Although several different types of aircraft were tried out in Europe toward the end of the nineteenth century, the Wright brothers, who experimented in their Dayton, Ohio, bicycle shop, were the first to succeed. On December 17, 1903, they took their fragile machine, which resembled a box kite, to the beach at Kitty Hawk, North Carolina, and with Orville at the controls, Wilbur spun the propeller until the engine caught; immediately the world's first motor-powered craft carrying a human being rose and flew for twelve seconds before settling down on the sand. On the fourth flight that day, Wilbur managed to keep their airplane up for fifty-nine seconds and traveled 852 feet. Six years later the U.S. Army contracted for Wright airplanes, which proved to be the forerunner of all subsequent aircraft, including today's massive jets.

## Change and More Change

Air transportation has its good and bad times, its advantages and drawbacks. Actually, the airlines have expanded and contracted their operations in the past like an accordion. However, in 1982 the changes became more extreme. For the first time, a major carrier shut down altogether when Braniff Airlines suspended all operations. At the same time, American Airlines announced that lack of business had forced it to suspend service to Columbus, Ohio, and Louisville, Kentucky, two cities it had served for more than half a century. Much worse were the stories circulating that the globe-circling giant, Pan American World Airways, was in serious trouble and could become a second Braniff. Shortly thereafter Pan Am paid off its employees and sold its airplanes. Later, Eastern Air Lines disappeared into a cut-rate line, threatening pension and other benefits for longtime loyal employees. What was wrong? What had happened to cause these problems?

Not only had fuel costs skyrocketed, but the nation's economy had started to sag and then spun into a recession in 1981. That same year, a strike by the Professional Air Traffic Controllers Organization caused the industry great harm. The federal government fired all strikers who did not return to work by a deadline set by President Ronald Reagan. Thereafter all airlines were forced to cut their schedules because fewer traffic controllers were manning the control towers. The airlines carried fewer passengers due to the recession and were forced at times to cut scheduled trips. This, however, was not the entire story.

From 1938 to 1978, the nation's airlines were regulated by the Civil Aeronautics Board, which decided the routes each company could fly and the fares it could charge and also regulated many other aspects of the business. In 1978 Congress enacted a law that deregulated the airlines and, in effect, gave them the freedom to fly where they chose and to charge whatever they wished, within certain limitations.

The immediate result of this change was that many new companies sprang up, giving tough competition to the older carriers and forcing them to reduce their rates and change their routes. As fares kept falling, so did profits, until most of the companies were operating in the red. So what had once been a generally thriving industry was now reporting one deficit after another. Employees received layoff notices, schedules were cut, services were discontinued, and airplanes were left parked at the far end of airports. One bad report followed another, but the picture was not altogether black.

Airline management teams were taking a fresh look at their businesses and coming up with new ideas. By implementing some innovative plans, the airlines realized more success than they had in several years. Air travel in the United States grew at a rapid pace until 2001, expanding from 172 million passengers in 1970 to nearly 642 million in 2003. However, over the next three years, a combination of factors, including the events of September 11, 2001, and an economic recession, combined to reduce traffic to 1996 levels. Yet despite this decline, air travel has remained one of our most popular modes of transportation.

## Types of Airlines

Several classes of airlines function in the United States. As of 2004 there were fifteen major airlines—twelve passenger and three cargo—which the U.S. Department of Transportation defines as having operating revenues of more than $1 billion. The largest of these, often called the *Big Six* (American, Continental, Delta, Northwest, United, and US Airways), generally have a "hub" and also fly internationally. A hub is a centrally located airport designated by an airline to receive a large number of its flights from many locations, and passengers can transfer from the hub to flights to any of the locations served by the airline's system. This hub-and-spoke system allows the carrier to serve the greatest number of passengers from as many locations as possible. For example, instead of flying five planes directly from New York to Atlanta, Birmingham, Jacksonville, Mobile, and St. Petersburg, an airline would fly from New York only to Atlanta—the hub. There, other local planes—the spokes—would be scheduled for each of the other cities. The system is not as convenient for passengers because they must change planes, but it reduces the number of trips and saves money. For some carriers the concept has great advantages.

In competition with the Big Six are low-cost, low-fare carriers, such as Southwest or Air Tran. These airlines have traditionally not used hub-and-spoke systems, instead offering flights between limited numbers of cities. They primarily focus on flying shorter routes (four hundred miles or fewer) and on serving leisure travelers. But some low-fare carriers are expanding their routes to include longer transcontinental and nonstop flights, which has allowed them to serve more business travelers.

Another type of passenger airline carrier is the commuter or regional carrier. As of 2004, there were approximately seventy-five of these carriers in operation. Regional airlines operate short- and medium-haul scheduled airline service connecting smaller communities with larger cities and with hubs. Some of the largest regional carriers are subsidiaries of the major airlines, but most are independently owned, often contracting their services to the majors. The regional airlines' fleet consists primarily of smaller nineteen- to sixty-eight-seat turboprop and forty- to seventy-seat jet aircraft. These regional airlines are the fastest-growing segment of commercial aviation, with one out of every seven domestic passengers flying on a regional airline during at least part of his or her trip.

Air cargo is another sector of the airline industry. Cargo can be carried in cargo holds of passenger airlines or on aircraft designed exclusively to carry freight. Cargo carriers do not provide door-to-door service. Instead, they provide only air transport from an airport near the cargo's origin to one near its destination.

Since airlines are here to stay, they must have people to run them, and most carriers will continue to offer good career opportunities to interested young men and women. The nature of the airline business makes it in some ways the most complicated of those in the transportation industry and, therefore, one with the greatest number of different jobs. Many jobs call for specialized training. For the purpose of reviewing the employment opportunities within the brief space available here, let's divide the business into two broad categories: airline operations and airline management. All jobs mentioned here call for at least a high school education. If additional education or training is required, that will be mentioned as well.

## Operating the Airline

Although pilots and flight attendants are the most visible occupations in this industry, two-thirds of all employees in air transportation work in ground occupations. Read the following job descriptions to see if one of these careers may be right for you.

### Passenger Service Personnel

A reservation and transportation ticket agent is most often the first employee that passengers meet after entering the airport. Ticket agents work at airport ticket counters and boarding gates and use computers to provide customer service to incoming passengers. They can make and confirm reservations, sell tickets, and issue boarding passes. They also work in call centers, answering phone inquiries about flight schedules and fares, verifying reservations, issuing tickets, and handling payments.

Customer service representatives assist passengers, check tickets when passengers board or disembark from an airplane, and check luggage at the reception area and ensure that it is placed on the proper carrier. They assist the elderly, persons with disabilities, and unaccompanied children in claiming personal belongings and baggage and in getting on and off the plane. They also may provide assistance to passengers who become ill or injured.

## Ramp Service Employees

The ramp service employees are those all-important men and women who perform the innumerable ground duties necessary to keep the airline flying. It is they who swarm over and through an airplane that has completed its trip and must be cleaned and serviced for its next flight. They lift the baggage off the conveyor, sort it, and place it on the various carts, each marked for a different departure. They also unload baggage from incoming planes and see that it reaches the baggage claim room where passengers locate and retrieve their own luggage. It is they who load and unload mail, freight, and express. Finally, it is they who drive the food service trucks, mechanized equipment, and fuel trucks as well as assist with fueling the aircraft.

A ramp service employee, assigned to driving the various pieces of equipment, must have a driver's license and, in some cases, a chauffeur's license. Those who handle luggage, express, and freight should also be in good health and have the physical strength needed to lift heavy bags and boxes.

## Mechanics

Aircraft mechanics and service technicians service, inspect, and repair planes. They may work on several different types of aircraft, such as jet transports, small propeller-driven airplanes, or helicopters. Many mechanics and technicians specialize, working on the airframe (the body of the aircraft) or the power plant (the engines) or avionics (the parts of an aircraft that depend on electronics, such as navigation and communication equipment). In small, independent repair shops, they usually inspect and repair many different types of aircraft.

Some mechanics and technicians specialize in scheduled maintenance required by the Federal Aviation Administration (FAA). Following a schedule based on the number of hours flown, calendar days, cycles of operation, or a combination of these factors, mechanics inspect the engines, landing gear, instruments, and other parts of aircraft and perform necessary maintenance and repairs.

When hiring aircraft mechanics, employers prefer graduates of aircraft mechanic trade schools, particularly those who gained experience in the military and are certified. Additionally, employers prefer mechanics who are in good physical condition and able to perform a variety of tasks. Aircraft mechanics must keep up to date on the latest technical changes and improvements in aircraft and associated systems. Most remain in the maintenance field, but they may advance to lead mechanic and, sometimes, to crew chief or shop supervisor.

Most mechanics who work on civilian aircraft are certified by the FAA as an "airframe mechanic" or a "power plant mechanic." Those who also have an inspector's authorization can certify work completed by other mechanics and perform required inspections. Uncertified mechanics are supervised by those with certificates.

The FAA requires at least eighteen months of work experience for an airframe or power plant certificate. For a combined A&P certificate, at least thirty months of experience working with both engines and airframes is required. Completion of a program at an FAA-certified mechanic school can substitute for the work experience requirement. Applicants for all certificates must pass written and oral tests and demonstrate that they can do the work authorized by the certificate. To obtain an inspector's authorization, a mechanic must have held an A&P certificate for at least three years, with twenty-four months of hands-on experience. Most airlines require that mechanics have a high school diploma and an A&P certificate.

Although a few people become mechanics through on-the-job training, most learn their job in one of approximately 170 trade schools certified by the FAA. About one-third of these schools award two-year and four-year degrees in avionics, aviation technology, or aviation maintenance management.

FAA standards established by law require that certified mechanic schools offer students a minimum of nineteen hundred actual class hours. Course work in schools normally lasts from eighteen to twenty-four months and provides training with the tools and equipment used on the job. Aircraft trade schools are placing more emphasis on technologies such as turbine engines, composite materials—including graphite, fiberglass, and boron—and aviation electronics, which are increasingly being used in the construction of new aircraft. Additionally, employers prefer mechanics who can perform a variety of tasks.

## Operations Office Employees

Airlines also require many behind-the-scenes professionals to keep operations running smoothly. The station manager is the overall administrator responsible for the entire company operation at the airport. He or she has earned this assignment after several years spent in various positions, perhaps starting his or her career as an aircraft cleaner.

## Flight Dispatchers

These professionals determine how each plane will reach its destination on time at the least operating cost but with the maximum load of passengers and cargo. Dispatchers must take into consideration such factors as temperature, amount of fuel loaded, number of passengers booked, weight of the freight to be stowed in the cargo compartment, head winds, and weather at the plane's destination. Computers give much of this information, but it takes an alert mind to put the information together in conference with the meteorologist and the flight crews to determine the best flight plan. Flight dispatchers must have a Federal Aviation Administration dispatcher's license and generally have moved up from jobs such as dispatch clerk, junior flight dispatcher, radio operator, meteorologist, or manager of a small station.

## Schedule Coordinators

These employees keep track of all aircraft and crews coming into or leaving the airport. If an airplane is delayed, it is the job of the coordinator to inform everyone concerned about the change. When an airplane has to be taken out of service, he or she must order a substitute, which may mean checking out other flights or canceling another flight if no backup plane is available. Whenever an extra airplane is needed, the schedule coordinator must first take into consideration what servicing or maintenance may be required and whether there is enough legal flight time left for the aircraft to fly before its next regular maintenance overhaul.

But there is more to the job. A coordinator handles crew scheduling and must know who is sick, on vacation, or having a day off, as well as who has the most seniority. It is also impossible to schedule a pilot for a New York–Chicago run if that pilot has been authorized to fly only on a New York–Houston run. The schedule coordinator must have had considerable experience in the operations office before he or she is assigned to this demanding post.

## Meteorologists

Meteorologists who assist in plotting flight plans have a college degree with a major in meteorology and may even have had experience with the U.S. Weather Bureau or a military weather service.

## Radio Operators

Radio operators converse with crews of flights in progress. They are always on duty ready to maintain contact with all planes to give and receive messages as the aircraft proceed to their destinations. These operators have had special training in technical schools and have obtained their radio operators' licenses from the Federal Communications Commission.

## Food Service Jobs

The food service sector of the airline industry includes such titles as pantry worker, dishwasher, salad maker, baker, steward chef, commissary chef, chief chef, supervisor, and assistant buyer. High school graduates who can obtain a health certificate will find this a good place to start their careers in food service because they will receive on-the-job training and with the right interest and aptitude, can advance to higher positions.

## Flight Crew

The employees that most air travelers are familiar with and pay most attention to are the members of the flight crew. Since pilots and flight attendants are the ones actually taking passengers to their destinations, the requirements for these positions are strict.

### Pilots

Except on small aircraft, two pilots usually make up the cockpit crew. Generally, the more experienced pilot, the captain, is in command and supervises all other crew members. The pilot and the copilot, often called the first officer, share flying and other duties, such as communicating with air traffic controllers and monitoring the instruments. Some large aircraft have a third pilot, the flight engineer, who monitors and operates many of the instruments and systems, making minor in-flight repairs and watching for other aircraft. The flight engineer also assists the pilots with the company, air traffic control, and cabin crew communications. However, new technologies are used to perform many flight tasks, and virtually all new aircraft now fly with only two pilots, who rely more heavily on computerized controls.

Pilots must have a commercial pilot's license with an instrument rating, must have a medical certificate, and must be certified to fly the types of aircraft that their employer operates. For example, helicopter pilots must hold a commercial pilot's certificate with a helicopter rating. Pilots receive their flight training from the military or from civilian flying schools. Strict physical requirements include passing a medical exam from an FAA-designated physician, having 20/20 vision and good hearing, and excellent general health.

Airlines generally require two years of college and increasingly prefer or require a college degree. Initial training for airline pilots includes a week of company indoctrination, three to six weeks of ground school and simulator training, and twenty-five hours of initial operating experience, including a check-ride with an FAA aviation safety inspector. Once trained, pilots are required to attend training and simulator checks once or twice a year throughout their careers.

Many pilots start as flight instructors, building up their flying hours while they earn money teaching. As they become more experienced, they occasionally fly charter planes or perhaps get jobs with small air transportation firms, such as air-taxi companies. Some advance to flying corporate planes. A small number get flight engineer jobs with the airlines. In the airlines, advancement usually depends on seniority provisions of union contracts.

## Flight Attendants

Airlines prefer to hire poised, tactful, and resourceful people who can interact comfortably with strangers and remain calm under duress to work as flight attendants. Applicants usually must be at least eighteen to twenty-one years old, although some carriers may have higher minimum-age requirements. Flight attendants must have excellent health and the ability to speak clearly. All U.S. airlines require that applicants be citizens of the United States or registered aliens with legal rights to obtain employment in the United States; Canadian airlines require flight attendants to be citizens of Canada.

Airlines usually have physical and appearance requirements. There are height requirements for reaching overhead bins, which often contain emergency equipment, and most airlines want candidates with weight proportionate to height. Men must have their hair cut above the collar and be clean shaven. Airlines prefer applicants with no visible tattoos, body piercing, or unusual hairstyles or makeup.

A high school diploma is the minimum educational requirement. However, airlines increasingly prefer applicants with a college degree and with experience in dealing with the public. Applicants who attend schools and colleges that offer flight attendant training may have an advantage over others. Flight attendants for international airlines generally must speak a foreign language fluently. For their international flights, some of the major airlines prefer candidates who can speak two major foreign languages.

In addition to education and training, airlines conduct a thorough background check as required by the FAA, which goes back as many as ten years. Employment is contingent on a successful background check. An applicant will not be offered a job or will be immediately dismissed if his or her background check shows any discrepancies.

Once hired, all candidates must undergo a period of formal training, ranging from three to eight weeks. After completing initial training, flight attendants are assigned to one of their airline's bases. New flight attendants are placed on reserve status and are called either to staff extra flights or to fill in for crewmembers who are sick, on vacation, or rerouted. When they are not on duty, reserve flight attendants must be available to report for flights on short notice. They usually remain on reserve for at least one year, but in some cities, it may take five to ten years or longer to advance from reserve status. Advancement takes longer today than in the past because experienced flight attendants are remaining in this career longer than they used to.

Some flight attendants become supervisors or take on additional duties, such as recruiting and instructing. Their experience also may qualify them for airline-related jobs involving contact with the public, such as reservation ticket agent or public relations specialist.

## Airline Management

In contrast to the intense activity at the airport, the dignified airline management offices located in a city skyscraper at first seem almost uninteresting, if not dull. The impression is erroneous, though, for the more we learn about what goes on within these walls, which are so remote from the airplanes, the more fascinating it all becomes.

### *Reservations*

This is where all of the incoming telephone calls and Web inquiries requesting information or reservations are received by numerous reservations agents, each of whom works within a tiny cubicle. Apart from a headset, a copy of the company's schedules and tariffs, and the *Official Airline Guide*, which contains schedules of all the airlines, the only other equipment in the cubicle is the computer terminal. This is connected to the reservations computer center, which may be located in another city.

When a passenger requests a seat on a certain flight, the agent asks the computer if there is space on that particular flight. The answer is flashed back instantly. Then the agent is able to make the reservation by typing the date, flight number, destination, and the passenger's name, address, and telephone number. This information is stored in the computer. Later it will be retrieved when it is time to see how many passengers are booked for that flight and a passenger manifest is prepared.

The reservations department and the ticket counter are two of the best places to start an airline career. Usually a week or ten days' classroom instruction in routings and fares is followed by three weeks of on-the-job training. Then, the agent is considered ready to work independently. The knowledge and experience gained in these positions give one an invaluable background for advancement.

## Sales

The reservations department is part of the general sales department. Although airlines depend for the most part on their newspaper, magazine, radio, and TV advertising as well as on the thousands of travel agents for their customers, a number of specialists are needed to handle various sales functions.

Following are the major divisions that make up an airline's sales department:

- **Passenger sales division.** This division is responsible for planning and carrying out sales programs.
- **Freight sales division.** This is the same as passenger sales, but for freight.
- **Reservations and ticket offices division.** This division oversees the operation of all reservations and ticket offices, planning and opening new offices, and training new employees.
- **Interline sales division.** This area encourages other airlines to route as much business as possible on each other's planes.
- **Agency sales division.** This division plans programs designed to increase the cooperation of travel agencies in booking business with the airline.

- **Convention sales division.** This section contacts organizations that will be holding large conventions and persuades convention delegates to use the airline.
- **Tariff division.** This area computes and publishes all of the company's fares and freight tariffs.
- **Schedule division.** This division prepares and publishes all the schedules for both the passenger planes and airfreighters that the company will operate.
- **Advertising division.** This section prepares and places all company advertising.

Many employees in the sales department have transferred from the reservations and ticket offices division. Others are college graduates with backgrounds in transportation, economics, statistics, business administration, or computer systems.

## Public Relations

The mission of this department is to provide the public with information about the company while at the same time promoting the company's image. Whenever an airline has a problem that is newsworthy enough to make the TV newscast or headlines, the public relations department must see that the airline receives sympathetic treatment.

In general, the PR staff spends its time promoting the airline to the public. However, if the carrier is involved in an accident, all efforts switch to toning down the news reports and trying to ensure that media coverage is factual and free of sensationalism.

For other than clerical positions, airlines generally look for applicants with college degrees in public relations or journalism.

## Purchasing

Airlines spend millions of dollars each year on everything from office supplies to jet craft. Most of the buying is done by purchasing agents or buyers. College degrees are necessary for good positions, and beginning jobs require that you have at least taken an associate degree program in purchasing. New employees are assigned to work with a senior member of the department.

## Finance

In the large finance department, auditors, statisticians, financial analysts, economists, clerks, and section and department heads are busy trying to keep track of the millions of dollars that flow in and out of the office each day from the innumerable ticket offices and freight depots.

The two most important sections of any airline finance department are revenue accounting, which keeps track of all incoming money, and disbursements, which pays all the bills. Closely associated with disbursements is the payroll section, responsible for preparing thousands of weekly and biweekly paychecks.

The staff of the insurance division is concerned with handling every type of insurance from the multimillion-dollar coverage on the aircraft fleet and passengers to the group life or health insurance, which is available to all employees.

The tax division of the department is staffed by professionals who specialize in accounting procedures and tax laws. For a large airline, federal taxes alone can run into millions of dollars; other taxes are collected by cities, counties, and states where the company conducts business.

The employees in the budget division forecast income and expenses. They also review every departmental budget to make certain it is not too large in proportion to company assets.

Every section has its administrative support staff, including secretaries, typists, and accounting clerks, each of whom has the appropriate background for his or her assigned division. These administrative professionals perform a wide variety of duties, and the other more specialized positions call for men and women who have had college courses in economics, statistics, mathematics, or business administration. Those employees who have done graduate work or attended a business school qualify for the more responsible posts, many of which lead to top management positions.

### Other Home Office Departments

Airlines own little or no property. They lease their office space and rent hangars as well as all of the lobbies, concourses, ticket counter areas, and offices at airport terminals. Planning and supervising construction of hangars, ticket counters, office and other space; negotiating leases; and working closely with airport managements are the responsibilities of the properties department.

In the human resources department, various professionals are responsible for interviewing and hiring job applicants, keeping all of the personnel records, setting wage and salary scales, negotiating contracts with labor unions, and handling employee benefits.

Last but not least is the mail room, where unskilled employees sort and stamp mail, wrap packages, and pack mail sacks for delivery to the post office. This is an ideal place for those just out of high school to start. Many an airline executive began his or her career sorting and delivering mail.

## Finding Your Job

The websites of most airlines provide information about career possibilities. In addition to learning about available positions, you can find valuable information about corporate culture, job requirements, training opportunities, and benefits. Career sites such as monster.com also allow you to search for jobs within the industry. You can also find jobs posted in the help-wanted section of your major newspaper.

If you know anyone who works for an airline or who has a friend employed by one of the carriers, talk with him or her to obtain first-hand information. If possible, secure the name of someone in the personnel department whom you might contact directly by mail or in person.

Further information about the air transport industry may be obtained by contacting the Air Transport Association of America or one or more of the unions of airline workers (see the Appendix for contact information).

## Earnings

What kind of salary can you expect from these interesting airline careers? Following are some examples of average salaries in 2004, based on the most recent statistics available from the Bureau of Labor Statistics.

Reservation ticket agents and travel clerks had median annual earnings of $27,750. The middle 50 percent earned between $21,430 and $39,410. Those working exclusively in air transportation had average earnings of $31,750.

Median hourly earnings of aircraft mechanics and service technicians were about $21.77, with the majority earning between

$17.82 and $27.18. Avionics technicians had median earnings of $21.30 per hour, with most earning between $18.12 and $25.12. For flight attendants, median annual earnings were $43,440, and most earned between $31,310 and $67,590. According to data from the Association of Flight Attendants, beginning attendants had median earnings of about $15,552. However, beginning pay scales for flight attendants vary by carrier. New hires usually begin at the same pay scale regardless of experience, and all flight attendants receive the same future pay increases based on an established pay scale. Flight attendants receive extra compensation for increased hours. Further, some airlines offer incentive pay for working holidays and night and international flights and for taking positions that require additional responsibility or paperwork.

Earnings of aircraft pilots and flight engineers vary greatly depending on whether they work as airline or commercial pilots. Earnings of airline pilots are among the highest in the nation and depend on factors such as the type, size, and maximum speed of the plane and the number of hours and miles flown. For example, pilots who fly jet aircraft usually earn higher salaries than pilots who fly turboprops. Airline pilots and flight engineers may earn extra pay for night and international flights.

Median annual earnings of airline pilots, copilots, and flight engineers were $129,250.

Median annual earnings of commercial pilots were $53,870. Most earned between $37,170 and $79,390.

Airline pilots usually are eligible for life and health insurance plans. They also receive retirement benefits, and if they fail the FAA physical examination at some point in their careers, they get disability payments. In addition, pilots receive an expense allowance, or per diem, for every hour they are away from home. Some airlines also provide allowances to pilots for purchasing and cleaning their uniforms. As an additional benefit, pilots and their immediate families usually are entitled to free or reduced-fare transportation on their own and other airlines.

## Employment Outlook

Most sectors of the airline industry were in a downturn in 2002, with several passenger airlines having declared bankruptcy and others on the verge of doing so. After six relatively successful years in the late 1990s—years that had been fueled by an increase in passenger volume and a booming economy—the growth in airline passenger traffic began to slow in 2001, coinciding with the economic recession. After the tragic events of September 11, 2001, passenger traffic dropped steeply, causing airlines to cut flights, lay off workers, and park surplus aircraft. Although passenger volume has since recovered to some degree, the growth rate in the industry will likely continue to be depressed for several years. In 2006 there were several near-collisions on runways, and increased security measures led to long waits and confusing regulations.

As the low-fare airlines continue to compete and gain market share over the higher-cost major airlines, and as passenger traffic remains lower, managing costs has become more critical to the survival of some airlines. Labor costs are the airlines' largest cost component—amounting to over 40 percent of some airlines' operating costs—and reducing these costs is a key part of the recovery plans of several major airlines. Reducing costs usually involves getting the constituent labor groups to restructure their wages, benefits, and work rules while continuing to improve labor productivity.

The airline industry faces many future challenges. Airlines must focus on cost control, cash preservation, and cautious growth. The industry's goal is to be prepared to respond quickly to economic recovery. Passenger volume should slowly improve, but it will take longer for rapid employment growth to return to the air transportation industry.

Keep in mind, however, that the nation's economy depends on continued airline operations. A visit to any busy airport will confirm this, if you watch the planes loading and unloading not only streams of passengers but also tons of express packages, mail, and freight.

Safe and inexpensive air travel is one of our nation's greatest achievements. The industry is constantly striving to better its record. That's why you can depend on it; there can be a future in this challenging industry for you, too.

# 8

---

# UNDERGROUND PIPELINE EMPIRE

THE CHINESE BUILT the first known pipeline about one thousand years ago using bamboo pipes to carry natural gas for various purposes, including evaporating salt brine. One of the next recorded uses of pipes was a Roman gravity water supply system of almost four hundred miles that brought water over aqueducts and through pipes to Rome. Pumps were used in 1582 to propel London's water supply through the city. Most early pipes were constructed of wood, which surely led to considerable leakage at joints due to rot and ground settling. Today cities throughout the world use metal and concrete pipes to bring water from distant points and distribute it to a wide variety of users.

As growing cities must reach out farther and farther to tap new water sources, pipelines become longer and longer. The huge pipeline that brings Colorado River water all the way to Los Angeles is a good example. (Although transporting gas and petroleum is our chief interest here, you should be aware of job opportunities in cities and towns that must obtain water from outside sources and distribute it. Inquire at your local water department about possible employment opportunities.)

Oil and natural gas furnish about three-fifths of our energy needs, fueling our homes, workplaces, factories, and transportation systems. In addition, they constitute the raw materials for plastics, chemicals, medicines, fertilizers, and synthetic fibers. Petroleum, commonly referred to as oil, is a natural fuel formed from the decay of plants and animals buried beneath the ground, under tremendous heat and pressure, for millions of years. Formed by a similar process, natural gas often is found in separate deposits and is sometimes mixed with oil.

Pipelines provide the cheapest and most efficient method of overland transportation. Because they are laid mostly underground, the pipes are subjected to very little wear and tear, since they are protected not only from the elements but also from vandalism. The power sources, pumps, and compressors are stationary, and piping is free of the unprofitable "return trip" required of railroad cars, trucks, and ships. Pipelines do not require handling, containers, terminals, or the need to keep extra vehicles or boats on hand to cover a breakdown or other emergency.

## Oil and Gas Extraction Process

Using a variety of methods both on land and at sea, small crews of specialized workers search for geologic formations that are likely to contain oil and gas. Sophisticated equipment and advances in computer technology have increased the productivity of exploration and revolutionized the process. Computers and advanced software analyze seismic data to provide three-dimensional models of subsurface rock formations. This technique lowers the risk involved in exploring by allowing scientists to locate and identify structural oil and gas reservoirs and the best locations to drill. Four-D, or "time-lapsed," seismic technology tracks the movement of fluids over time and enhances production performance even further. Another method of searching for oil and gas is based on collecting and ana-lyzing core samples of rock, clay, and sand in the earth's layers.

After scientific studies indicate the possible presence of oil, an oil company selects a well site and installs a towerlike steel struc-ture called a *derrick* to support the drilling equipment. A hole is drilled deep into the earth until oil or gas is found; if none is located, the company abandons the effort. Similar techniques are employed in offshore drilling, except that the drilling equipment is part of a steel platform that either sits on the ocean floor or floats on the surface and is anchored to the ocean floor.

In rotary drilling, a rotating bit attached to a length of hollow drill pipe bores a hole in the ground by chipping and cutting rock. As the bit cuts deeper, more pipe is added. A stream of drilling *mud* (a mixture of clay, chemicals, and water) is continuously pumped through the drill pipe and through holes in the drill bit to cool the drill bit, plaster the walls of the hole to prevent cave-ins, carry crushed rock to the surface, and prevent blowouts by equalizing pressure inside the hole. When a drill bit wears out, all drill pipe must be removed from the hole a section at a time, the bit replaced, and the pipe returned to the hole. New materials and better designs have advanced drill bit technology, permitting faster, more cost-effective drilling for longer periods.

When oil or gas is found, the drill pipe and bit are pulled from the well, and metal pipe (casing) is lowered into the hole and cemented in place. The upper end of the casing is fastened to a system of pipes and valves called a *wellhead*, through which natural pressure forces the oil or gas into separation and storage tanks. Pumps are used if there is not sufficient natural pressure to force the oil to the surface. In some cases, water, steam, or gas may be injected into the oil-producing formation to improve recovery.

Crude oil is transported to refineries by pipeline, ship, barge, truck, or railroad. Natural gas usually is transported to processing plants by pipeline. Oil refineries may be thousands of miles away from the producing fields, but gas processing plants typically are near the fields, so that impurities such as water, sulfur, and natural gas liquids can be removed before the gas is piped to customers.

## Transportation Occupations in the Industry

People with many different skills are needed to explore for oil and gas, drill new wells, maintain existing wells, and process natural gas. The largest group, construction and extraction workers, account for about 37 percent of industry employment. Professional and related workers account for about 14 percent of industry employment, and managerial, business, and financial workers account for about 12 percent. Transportation and material moving workers make up about 10 percent, and production workers about 9 percent.

In the case of oil and gas, transportation is slightly different from the way we have considered it so far in this book. In this industry, the pipelines themselves are the modes of transportation for the extracted substances. For this reason, those workers who construct, install, and operate the pipelines can fall under the heading of transportation workers for our purposes.

Exploration operations are led by a petroleum geologist, who analyzes and interprets the information gathered. The exploration team may also include other geological specialists, such as paleontologists and mineralogists, as well as surveyors and drafters who map the activities.

Once a potential drill site has been located, petroleum engineers plan and supervise the actual drilling operation. Drilling superintendents serve as supervisors of drilling crews, overseeing one or more drilling rigs.

Rotary drilling crews usually consist of four or five workers. Rotary drillers supervise the crew and operate machinery that controls drilling speed and pressure. Rotary-rig engine operators are responsible for the engines that provide the power for drilling and hoisting. Second in charge, derrick operators work on small platforms high on rigs to help run pipe in and out of well holes and operate the pumps that circulate mud through the pipe. Rotary-driller helpers, also known as roughnecks, guide the lower ends of pipe to well openings and connect pipe joints and drill bits.

Though not necessarily part of the drilling crew, roustabouts, or general laborers, do general oil-field maintenance and construction work, such as cleaning tanks and building roads.

Pumpers and their helpers operate and maintain the motors, pumps, and other surface equipment that forces oil from wells and regulate the flow, according to a schedule set up by petroleum engineers and production supervisors. In fields where oil flows under natural pressure and does not require pumping, switchers open and close valves to regulate the flow. Gaugers measure and record the flow, taking samples to check quality. Treaters test the oil for water and sediment and remove these impurities by opening a drain or using special equipment. In most fields, pumping, switching, gauging, and treating operations are automatic.

Other skilled oil-field workers include oil well cementers, who mix and pump cement into the space between the casing and well walls to prevent cave-ins; acidizers, who pump acid down the well and into the producing formation to increase oil flow; and perforator operators, who use subsurface "guns" to pierce holes in the casing to make openings for oil to flow into the well bore. Sample-taker operators take samples of soil and rock formations from wells to help geologists determine the presence of oil; and well pullers remove pipes, pumps, and other subsurface devices from wells for cleaning, repairing, and salvaging.

Many other skilled workers, including welders, pipe fitters, electricians, and machinists, are employed in maintenance operations to install and repair pumps, gauges, pipes, and other equipment.

In addition to the types of workers required for onshore drilling, crews at offshore locations also need radio operators, cooks, ships' officers, sailors, and pilots. These workers make up the support personnel who work on or operate drilling platforms, crew boats, barges, and helicopters.

Most workers involved in gas processing are operators. Gas treaters tend automatically controlled treating units that remove water and other impurities from natural gas. Gas-pumping-station operators tend compressors that raise the pressure of gas for transmission in pipelines. Both types of workers can be assisted by gas-compressor operators.

Many employees in large natural gas processing plants, such as welders, electricians, instrument repairers, and laborers, perform maintenance activities. In contrast, many small plants are automated and are checked at periodic intervals by maintenance workers or operators, or monitored by instruments that alert operators if trouble develops. In nonautomated plants, workers usually combine the skills of both operators and maintenance workers.

## Job Qualifications and Training

A variety of educational backgrounds will qualify you for work in the oil and gas pipeline industry, depending on the type of job you are looking for. The most common entry-level field jobs, such as roustabouts or roughnecks, usually require little or no previous training or experience, but you must be physically fit and pass a physical examination. You may also be required to take an aptitude test and undergo screening for drug use.

You can usually learn the basic skills over a period of days through on-the-job training. However, given the increasing complexity of operations and the sophisticated nature of technology used today, employers now demand a higher level of skill and adaptability, including the ability to work with computers and other sophisticated equipment.

For well operation and maintenance jobs, companies generally prefer applicants who live nearby, have mechanical ability, and possess knowledge of oil-field processes. Because this work offers the advantage of a fixed locale, members of drilling crews or exploration parties who prefer not to travel may transfer to well operation and maintenance jobs. Training is acquired on the job.

Promotion opportunities for some jobs may be limited because of the general decline of the domestic petroleum industry. Advancement opportunities for oil-field workers remain best for those who possess skill and experience. For example, roustabouts may move up to become switchers, gaugers, and pumpers. More experienced roughnecks may advance to derrick operators and, after several years, to drillers. Drillers may advance to tool pushers. There should continue to be some opportunities for entry-level field crew workers to acquire the skills that qualify them for the higher-level jobs within the industry. Because of the critical nature of the work, offshore crews, even those at the entry level, generally are more experienced than land crews. Many companies will not employ someone who has no knowledge of oil-field operations to work on an offshore rig, so workers who have gained experience as part of a land crew might advance to offshore operations.

The experience that you gain in many oil and gas extraction jobs can also be applied to other industries. For example, roustabouts can move to construction jobs, and machinery operators and repairers can transfer to other industries with similar machinery.

## Earnings

According to the most recent available information from the Bureau of Labor Statistics, the average earnings of workers in the oil and gas extraction industry were significantly higher than the average for all industries in 2004. The average hourly earnings of nonsupervisory workers in the oil and gas extraction sector were $18.58 compared with $15.67 for all workers in private industry. Due to the working conditions, employees at offshore operations generally earn higher wages than those at onshore oil fields. College-educated workers and technical school graduates in professional and technical occupations usually earn the most. Here is a breakdown of hourly wages based on job title:

First-line supervisors/managers of construction
    trades and extraction workers        $27.44
Petroleum pump system operators, refinery
    operators, and gaugers        $23.52
Wellhead pumpers        $16.73
Rotary drill operators        $16.17
Service unit operators        $15.87
Derrick operators        $15.26
Roustabouts        $12.60
Helpers/extraction workers        $11.58

## Employment Outlook

The oil and gas pipeline industry employed about 316,000 wage and salary workers in 2004. The majority work as contractors, while only four in ten are employed directly by the oil and gas extraction companies.

Although onshore oil and gas extraction companies are found in forty-two states, almost three out of four of the industry's workers are located in just four states: California, Louisiana, Oklahoma, and Texas. Although most workers are employed on land, many work at offshore sites, and many Americans are employed by oil companies at locations in Africa, the North Sea, the Far East, the Middle East, South America, and countries of the former Soviet Union.

In Canada, where petroleum production is a major industry, most exploration and production occurs in Alberta, with a significant number of operations in British Columbia and Saskatchewan. Drilling from large offshore platforms occurs on the Newfoundland continental shelf. In 2005 almost twenty-five thousand new oil wells were drilled in Canada. Daily, more than one hundred new wells are drilled in Alberta alone.

In general, the level of future crude petroleum and natural gas exploration and development, and therefore, employment opportunities in this industry, remains contingent on the size of accessible reserves available and the going prices for oil and gas. Stable and favorable prices are needed to allow companies enough revenue to expand exploration and production projects to keep pace with growing global energy demand, particularly by India and China. Rising worldwide demand for oil and gas is likely to cause higher long-term prices and generate the needed incentive to continue exploring and developing oil and gas in this country, at least in the short run. Over the moderate term, fewer reserves of oil and gas in North America will cause a decline in domestic production, unless new oil and gas fields are found and developed.

Environmental concerns, accompanied by strict regulation and limited access to protected federal lands, also continue to have a major impact on this industry. Restrictions on drilling in environmentally sensitive areas and other environmental constraints should continue to limit exploration and development, both onshore and offshore. However, changes in policy could expand exploration and drilling for oil and natural gas in currently protected areas, especially in Alaska.

Although some new oil and gas deposits are being discovered in this country, companies increasingly are moving to more lucrative foreign locations. As companies expand into other areas around the globe, the need for employees in the United States is reduced. However, advances in technology have increased the proportion of exploratory wells that yield oil and gas, enhanced offshore exploration and drilling capabilities, and extended the production of existing wells. As a result, more exploration and development ventures are profitable and provide employment opportunities that otherwise would have been lost.

Despite an overall decline in employment in the oil and gas extraction industry, job opportunities in most occupations should be good. Employment opportunities will be best for those who have previous experience and technical skills, especially qualified professionals and extraction workers who have significant experience in oil field operations and who can work with new technologies— such as three-D and four-D seismic exploration methods, horizontal and directional drilling techniques, and deepwater and subsea technologies—as employers develop and implement sophisticated new equipment.

# 9

---

# WORKING FOR THE GOVERNMENT

Do you know that the largest employer in the United States, if not the world, is the federal government, which employs nearly two million civilian workers? There are also state, county, and municipal governments, to say nothing of the many public authorities, some of which operate transportation systems. The number of men and women working for the government falls between 3.5 and 4 million. Because transportation-related jobs are not numerous in the state, county, and municipal categories, you will find your best opportunities probably exist in U.S. worldwide operations.

## U.S. Military Service

Even though the new century ushered in a cutback in government expenditures and reduction in the number of government employees, certain functions must continue. The military received additional billions, while other government services were cut. The armed forces are the best place to start our survey of jobs because we have a military establishment made up of volunteers, and the door is wide open to young men and women who can qualify for admission. What makes military service so attractive is the opportunity to obtain vocational training. At a time when education is expensive and beyond the reach of many, it makes sense to investigate a career with one of the military services.

## Armed Forces

The four principal military services in the United States—Air Force, Army, Marines, and Navy—offer a wide range of career opportunities in clerical and administrative work, electrical and electronic occupations, and hundreds of other specialties, many of which are related to transportation.

Transportation is essential to all of the services. You may enlist in any one of a variety of programs that involve different combinations of active or reserve duty. Job training available to enlisted personnel may depend on the length of service commitment, general and technical aptitudes, personal preferences, and most of all, the needs of the service at that time.

It would be impossible to list all the career opportunities available in the various services. The following list is typical of transportation skills that are transferable to civilian positions if you should decide to resign from the service after completing your enlistment. You should bear in mind that the technological changes and needs of each service vary from time to time, so be sure to check into the training requirements before making a commitment.

Several areas of specialization exist within the transportation field for military personnel.

- **Aircraft maintenance:** aviation maintenance administration, aviation safety equipment, aviation structure mechanic, aviation hydraulic mechanic, basic helicopter course
- **Air traffic control and enlisted flight crews:** aerial navigator, airborne radio operator, air traffic controller
- **Avionics:** avionics technician, advanced first-term avionics, aviation electrician mate, precision measuring equipment technician, avionics technician intermediate
- **Electronics maintenance:** aviation radio technician, aviation radio repairer, meteorological equipment maintenance, aviation radar technician, ground radar technician, aviation fire control technician
- **Motor transport:** fuels and electrical systems repair, basic automotive mechanic, metal body repair, advanced automotive mechanic
- **Transportation:** defense advanced traffic management, installation traffic management

## U.S. Transportation Command (USTRANSCOM)

USTRANSCOM provides air, land, and sea transport for the Department of Defense (DoD) in both peace and time of war. It is responsible for the creation and implementation of world-class global deployment and distribution systems to support missions assigned by the president, secretary of defense, and combat commander.

In addition to depending on members of the military services, USTRANSCOM also relies on civilians employed by the Department of Defense and commercial partners to accomplish a wide range of joint mobility missions. The combination of people, trucks, trains, aircraft, ships, information systems, and infrastructure allow USTRANSCOM to operate the world's most responsive strategic mobility system.

USTRANSCOM currently controls a fleet of military assets valued in excess of $52 billion, including: 87 ships, 1,269 aircraft, 2,150 railcars and assorted equipment, and $1.4 billion in infrastructure, as well as access through its commercial partners to more than 1,001 aircraft and 360 vessels in the Civil Reserve Air Fleet (CRAF) and Voluntary Intermodal Sealift Agreement (VISA), respectively.

During an average week, USTRANSCOM conducts more than nineteen hundred air missions, with twenty-five ships under way and ten thousand ground shipments operating in 75 percent of the world's countries. As of October 2004 the command had moved more than 1.9 million passengers, 1,108,987 tons by air, 3.7 million tons by sea, and more than 53.7 billion barrels of fuel by ship.

USTRANSCOM's three component commands—the air force's Air Mobility Command, Scott AFB, Illinois; the navy's Military Sealift Command, Washington, DC; and the army's Military Surface Deployment and Distribution Command, Alexandria, Virginia—provide intermodal transportation across the spectrum of military operations.

### Air Mobility Command (AMC)

The Air Mobility Command of the U.S. Air Force provides strategic and tactical airlift, air refueling, and aeromedical evacuation services for deploying, sustaining, and redeploying U.S. forces wherever they are needed. Many special duty and operational support aircraft are also assigned to AMC (including Air Force One). In addition, AMC contracts with commercial air carriers for transportation of Department of Defense passengers and cargo.

Educational opportunities available through the air force include a degree from the Community College of the Air Force (CCAF) and technical training.

## Military Sealift Command (MSC)

The mission of the navy's Military Sealift Command is to provide ocean transportation of equipment, fuel, supplies, and ammunition to sustain U.S. forces worldwide during peacetime and in war. During a war, more than 95 percent of all equipment and supplies needed to sustain the U.S. military is carried by sea.

MSC, headquartered in Washington, DC, is a worldwide organization that employs more than eight thousand military and civilian personnel. The command is responsible for ocean transportation of military supplies and equipment, for providing seagoing platforms to support special at-sea missions, and for logistics support to U.S. Navy ships at sea.

The command has many different career opportunities both ashore and afloat. As part of its workforce, MSC employs more than four thousand civil service mariners, federal government employees who crew and sail MSC's Naval Fleet Auxiliary Force and special missions ships—all noncombatant ships.

## Surface Deployment and Distribution Command (SDDC)

The Surface Deployment and Distribution Command provides ocean terminal, commercial ocean liner, and traffic management services to deploy, sustain, and redeploy U.S. forces on a global basis. The SDDC is responsible for surface transportation and is the liaison between Department of Defense shippers and the commercial transportation carrier industry. This includes movement of DOD-member household goods and privately owned vehicles.

SDDC is the nation's largest customer to the moving industry, with more than half a million household goods moves a year. The command also provides transportation for troops and material to ports of departure in the United States and overseas and manages twenty-four ports worldwide, including military terminals at Sunny Point, North Carolina, and Concord, California.

## Requirements and Training

Requirements for each service vary, but certain qualifications for enlistment are common to all branches. To enlist, you must be between seventeen and thirty-five years old for active service, be a U.S. citizen or an alien holding permanent resident status, not have a felony record, and possess a birth certificate. Applicants who are aged seventeen must have the consent of a parent or legal guardian before entering the service.

To join the armed forces as an enlisted member, you must sign an enlistment contract, which is a legal agreement that usually involves a commitment to eight years of service. Depending on the terms of the contract, two to six years are spent on active duty, and the balance is spent in the national guard or reserves. The enlistment contract obligates the service to provide the agreed-upon job, rating, pay, cash bonuses for enlistment in certain occupations, medical and other benefits, occupational training, and continuing education. In return you must serve satisfactorily for the period specified.

You will be required to pass a written examination and meet certain minimum physical standards, such as height, weight, vision, and overall health. All branches of the armed forces require high school graduation or its equivalent.

If you are thinking about enlisting in the military, it is a good idea to learn as much as you can about military life before making a decision—this is especially important if you are thinking about making the military a career. Speak to friends and relatives who have military experience. Find out what the military can offer you and what it will expect in return. Then talk to a recruiter, who can determine whether you qualify for enlistment, explain the various enlistment options, and tell you which military occupational specialties currently have openings. Bear in mind that the recruiter's job is to recruit promising applicants into his or her branch of military service, so the information that the recruiter gives you is likely to stress the positive aspects of military life in the branch in which he or she serves.

You can take the aptitude exam (Armed Services Vocational Aptitude Battery), which the military uses as a placement exam. The recruiter can schedule you for the exam without any obligation. Many high schools offer the exam as an easy way for students to explore the possibility of a military career, and the test also affords an insight into career areas in which the student has demonstrated aptitudes and interests.

If you decide to join the military, the next step is to pass the physical examination and sign an enlistment contract. Negotiating the contract involves choosing, qualifying for, and agreeing on a number of enlistment options, such as the length of active-duty time, which may vary according to the option.

Following enlistment, you will undergo basic training, or "boot camp." Following basic training, you will most likely have additional training at a technical school to prepare you for your military occupational specialty. The formal training period generally lasts from ten to twenty weeks.

Many service people get college credit for the technical training they receive on duty, which, combined with off-duty courses, can lead to an associate degree through programs in community colleges such as the Community College of the Air Force. In addition to on-duty training, military personnel may choose from a variety of educational programs. Most military installations have tuition assistance programs for people who wish to take courses during off-duty hours. The courses may be correspondence courses or courses in degree programs offered by local colleges or universities. Tuition assistance pays up to 100 percent of college costs up to a credit-hour and annual limit.

Each of the military services publishes handbooks, fact sheets, and pamphlets describing entrance requirements, training and advancement opportunities, and other aspects of military careers. These publications are widely available at all recruiting stations, at most state employment service offices, and in high schools, colleges, and public libraries. Information on educational and other veterans' benefits is available from U.S. Department of Veterans Affairs (VA) offices located throughout the country.

In addition, the Defense Manpower Data Center, an agency of the U.S. Department of Defense, publishes *Military Career Guide Online*, a compendium of military occupational, training, and career information designed for use by students and job seekers. This information is available at www.todaysmilitary.com.

## Earnings and Benefits

The VA provides numerous benefits to those who have served at least twenty-four months of continuous active duty in the armed forces. Veterans are eligible for free care in VA hospitals for all service-related disabilities, regardless of time served; those with other medical problems are eligible for free VA care if they are unable to pay the cost of hospitalization elsewhere. However, admission to a VA medical center depends on the availability of beds. Veterans also are eligible for certain loans, including loans to purchase a home. Veterans, regardless of health, can convert a military life insurance policy to an individual policy with any participating company upon separation from the military. In addition, job counseling, testing, and placement services are available.

Veterans who participate in the Montgomery GI Bill Program receive education benefits. Under this program, armed forces personnel may elect to deduct up to $100 a month from their pay during the first twelve months of active duty, putting the money toward their future education. Upon separation from active duty, the fund can be used to finance educational costs at any VA-approved institution. Among those institutions that are approved by the VA are many vocational, correspondence, certification, business, technical, and flight-training schools; community and junior colleges; and colleges and universities.

Enlisted personnel with fewer than four months' service time earned an average monthly salary of $1,142.70; those with more than four months earned $1,235.10. Those who entered service with advanced skills or education earned $1,612.80 per month.

In addition to receiving their basic pay, military personnel are provided with free room and board (or a tax-free housing and subsistence allowance), free medical and dental care, a military clothing allowance, military supermarket and department store shopping privileges, thirty days of paid vacation a year (referred to as *leave*), and travel opportunities. In many duty stations, military personnel may receive a housing allowance that can be used for off-base housing. This allowance can be substantial, but it varies greatly by rank and duty station.

## Canadian Military Service

With more than one hundred job options available, you can surely find a career in transportation with the Canadian military.

The Canadian Forces (CF) is the umbrella organization that covers three elements: the navy, the army, and the air force. Careers are available in the following areas:

- Administration and support
- Combat arms
- Engineering
- Health services
- Operators
- Reconnaissance and intelligence
- Technicians

To prepare for the many transportation opportunities that are available, the CF offers occupational and advanced training in numerous disciplines. Some of the CF schools that might be of interest are:

- Air navigation
- Military engineering
- Administration and logistics
- Electrical and mechanical engineering
- Communications and electronics
- Military intelligence
- Aerospace studies
- Flight training

You may begin a military career as a noncommissioned member (NCM). NCMs start out as recruits and are then trained to perform specific occupations in the CF. Some are trained as technicians to keep the equipment repaired; some are operators that use specific and complicated electrical and mechanical equipment; and some are users of general equipment. There are seventy-three NCM occupations available in the CF. Your training will be specific for the occupation in which you are enrolled.

Officers are trained to be responsible for a group of people. They oversee the sailors, soldiers, or air personnel in the conduct of their activities, whether on a base or aboard a ship. As an officer, you could serve in Canada or overseas. The CF offers thirty-two officer careers.

## Requirements and Training

To be eligible for consideration for the Canadian Forces, you must be a Canadian citizen; those with permanent resident status may be considered only under exceptional circumstances. You must be seventeen years of age (with parental/guardian consent) or older. The minimum education requirements vary, depending on your entry plan and/or occupation. For example, a tenth-grade education is sufficient for combat arms occupations, while a university degree is required for the direct entry officer plan.

The easiest and most direct way to apply for the Canadian Forces is to complete the online application. If you prefer not to do so, you have two alternatives. You may apply in person at your local recruiting center or reserve unit of your choice, or you may apply by mail, providing all necessary forms and supporting documents.

You will need to complete the CF Application Form; Personnel Screening, Consent and Authorization Form; and the References for Applicant Form. In addition, you must provide a birth certificate, citizenship card, original transcript of your educational record, and proof of trades or qualifications.

The Canadian Forces offers many education and training opportunities. Basic training for recruits and officer candidates is generally conducted at the Canadian Forces Leadership and Recruit School (CFLRS) in Saint-Jean-sur-Richelieu, Quebec, and its detachment in Borden, Ontario. During the fourteen-week program, you will learn the fundamentals of military knowledge and leadership through training that emphasizes physical and mental strength, basic military skills, and the elements of leadership and ethical values.

The Canadian Forces Aboriginal entry program provides Aboriginal people in Canada the opportunity to explore the Canadian Forces and experience basic training prior to deciding to enlist. The three-week pre-recruit training course incorporates elements of the basic training program combined with information on CF Aboriginal history and military occupation career counseling.

The Royal Military College of Canada (RMC), located in Kingston, Ontario, is a bilingual institution offering an education in the professional and personal skills needed for those in leadership positions. Graduates of RMC go on to pursue careers as officers in the Canadian Forces.

The Canadian Forces also provides continuing professional education at more than two dozen specialized schools that are located throughout the country. Those that might be of interest for transportation specialties include the Air Navigation School in Winnipeg, Manitoba; School of Military Engineering in Gagetown, New Brunswick; School of Administration and Logistics in Borden, Ontario; School of Aerospace Studies in Winnipeg; Flying Training School in Winnipeg; and the Air Command Academy, also in Borden.

## Earnings and Benefits

Your pay in the Canadian Forces will depend on your occupation and rank. All service personnel are paid on the same scale.

The 2007 the salary range for most jobs follows:

### Regular Force (Full-Time Employment)
Officer: $42,000 ($66,000 after five years)
Noncommissioned member: $30,000 ($50,000 after five years)

### Reserve Force (Part-Time Employment)
Officer: $92/day ($153/day after five years)
Noncommissioned member: $78/day ($117/day after five years)

Regular force personnel receive twenty working days of annual vacation leave until the completion of five years of service, after which annual leave is increased to twenty-five working days per year and continues to increase based on years of service. Members of the reserve force are entitled to one working day of vacation for each fifteen consecutive days of service, to a maximum of twenty-four working days in a leave year.

Members of the Canadian Forces participate in a pension plan and receive comprehensive medical and dental benefits. Maternity and parental leave benefits are also available to qualified female and male members.

# U.S. Coast Guard

The U.S. Coast Guard and Coast Guard Reserve, the fifth branch of the country's military service, falls under the jurisdiction of the Department of Homeland Security. Its primary responsibilities include:

- Search and rescue
- Maritime law enforcement
- Aids to navigation
- Ice breaking
- Environmental protection
- Port security
- Military readiness

As the country's oldest continuous seagoing service, the coast guard employs more than forty thousand active-duty personnel, eight thousand reservists, and thirty-five thousand auxiliary personnel who work in fields ranging from small-boat mechanics to electronics technicians. These men and women work to protect the public, the environment, and the nation's economic and security interests in any maritime region where those interests may be at risk, including international waters and America's coasts, ports, and inland waterways.

The coast guard offers many and varied career opportunities for enlisted personnel, officers, auxiliary personnel, and civilians. For complete information about careers, entry requirements, and training and benefits, visit the online recruitment site at www.gocoast guard.com.

# Canadian Coast Guard

The Canadian Coast Guard is part of Fisheries and Oceans Canada, the federal department responsible for developing and implementing policies and programs in support of the nation's economic, ecological, and scientific interests in oceans and inland waters.

The coast guard has five principal roles:

- Maritime safety
- Protection of the marine and freshwater environment
- Facilitation of maritime trade and commerce and maritime accessibility
- Support to marine science
- Support to Canada's federal maritime properties

Each coast guard role is composed of several mission areas, which in turn are based on one or more mandated or authorized duties. Many missions benefit more than one role. For example, while an aids-to-navigation mission supports the role of accessibility by facilitating the movement of people and goods, the system of aids also supports maritime safety and protection of the marine environment by preventing accidents. This interwoven, overlapping combination of roles and missions calls for coast guard resources that are similarly capable of running multiple missions.

Fleet vessels, for example, are constructed to be able to deliver a variety of programs, often concurrently. Unlike vessels that serve simply as a mode of transportation, moving goods or people from point A to point B, most fleet vessels are multitasked, and all are crewed with professionally trained mariners capable of delivering on-water programs. On any given day, a coast guard vessel and its specialized crew can be supporting a science undertaking while at the same time decommissioning buoys and serving as both a secondary search-and-rescue (SAR) vessel and a visible symbol of a Canadian presence in support of sovereignty.

For additional information about the Canadian Coast Guard, visit www.ccg-gcc.gc.ca.

## U.S. Customs and Border Protection

U.S. Customs and Border Protection is the agency responsible for assessing and collecting revenue on imported merchandise, enforcing customs and related laws, and ensuring the security of our nation's borders. As part of the Department of Homeland Security, it employs more than fifteen thousand workers, most of whom are located at the nearly three hundred ports of entry. A few are assigned to overseas posts.

The customs service enforces both its own as well as approximately four hundred laws and regulations for forty other federal agencies. It also conducts a variety of antismuggling programs.

Here are brief descriptions of the principal career positions with the service.

• **Customs inspectors.** Inspectors enforce laws governing imports and exports by inspecting cargo, baggage, and articles worn or carried by people, vessels, vehicles, trains, and aircraft entering or leaving the United States. They examine, count, weigh, gauge, measure, and sample commercial and noncommercial cargoes entering and leaving the United States. Customs inspectors seize prohibited or smuggled articles, intercept contraband, and apprehend, search, detain, and arrest violators of U.S. laws.

• **Customs agents.** Agents investigate violations, such as narcotics smuggling, money laundering, child pornography, and customs fraud, and they enforce the Arms Export Control Act. During domestic and foreign investigations, they develop and use informants, conduct physical and electronic surveillance, and examine records from importers and exporters, banks, couriers, and manufacturers. They conduct interviews, serve on joint task forces with other agencies, and get and execute search warrants.

• **Import specialists.** These employees are vital because of the unprecedented growth in world trade, new trade agreements, and increased trade complexity. These specialist agents interact with both importers and exporters and are responsible for decisions regarding a staggering variety of merchandise, manufactured goods, and commodities.

Import specialists are responsible for classifying and appraising a portion of the billions of dollars worth of commercially imported merchandise that enters the United States every year. They determine which products may legally enter the country by enforcing laws protecting public health and safety, intellectual property rights, fair trade practices, and the like. They may also play a key role in criminal enforcement team investigations of smuggling, commercial fraud, and counterfeiting.

Seven weeks of specialized training will enable import specialists to develop an expert knowledge of import and export trends, commodities, and industries, as well as complex international trade agreements. The position requires intellect, discipline, organizational abilities, and analytical skills.

- **Customs patrol officers.** These officers carry out the difficult task of detecting and apprehending violators of the four hundred statutes enforced by the service. They prevent smuggling into the country and may serve anywhere in the United States from along the frozen northern border to the deserts of the Southwest, from urban waterfronts to secluded coastlines. No two assignments are alike, nor are any two working days.
- **Customs aides.** Aides perform semitechnical duties that require some specialized knowledge of the provisions of customs laws and regulations. They assist inspectors and other specialists in the service.

There are some other interesting career possibilities available with the service, too.

- Canine enforcement officers train and use dogs to enforce customs laws pertaining to the smuggling of marijuana, narcotics, and dangerous drugs.
- Customs pilots are part of a program of air surveillance of illegal traffic crossing U.S. borders by air, land, or sea. Pilots also apprehend, arrest, and search violators of customs and related laws.
- Customs chemists play an important part in protecting the nation's health and safety as well as the security of the country's commerce. They are called upon to analyze imported merchandise ranging from textile fibers to contraband narcotics.

In addition to these specialist positions, there are numerous data processing positions in the Washington, DC, headquarters, to say nothing of the usual clerical openings.

Customs jobs are filled and administered under the competitive civil service system. Since the educational and experience requirements for each of the jobs vary, it is best to check with the nearest Federal Job Information Center or the customs service to learn about openings and what the requirements are for each.

For more information visit www.cbp.gov.

## Canada Border Services Agency

Canada's Border Services Agency employs people at hundreds of locations across the country. These professionals work to keep restricted goods and people from entering the country, help locate missing children, and protect Canada from illegal drugs and weapons.

In addition to the position of customs inspector and other professional titles, the Canada Border Services Agency also offers employment opportunities for students. As a Student Border Services Officer, you can earn an hourly wage working part-time during the school year or full-time in summer. The Federal Student Work Experience Program employs seven thousand students annually in temporary jobs among various federal agencies; co-op and internship programs are also available.

## Air Traffic Control

The air traffic control system is a vast network of people and equipment that ensures the safe operation of commercial and private aircraft. Air traffic controllers coordinate the movement of air traffic to make certain that planes stay a safe distance apart. Although their immediate concern is safety, controllers also must direct planes efficiently to minimize delays. Some regulate airport traffic through designated airspaces; others regulate airport arrivals and departures. Here are some more detailed descriptions of various air traffic control positions.

- **Airport tower controllers or terminal controllers.** These are the controllers who watch over all planes traveling through the airport's airspace. Their main responsibility is to organize the flow of aircraft into and out of the airport. Relying on radar and visual observation, they closely monitor each plane to ensure a safe distance between all aircraft and to guide pilots between the hangar or ramp and the end of the airport's airspace. In addition, controllers keep pilots informed about changes in weather conditions, such as wind shear, which is a sudden change in the velocity or direction of the wind that can cause the pilot to lose control of the aircraft.
- **En route controllers.** After each plane departs, airport tower controllers notify en route controllers who will next take charge. There are twenty air route traffic control centers located around the country, each employing three hundred to seven hundred controllers, with more than 150 on duty during peak hours at the busiest facilities.

Airplanes usually fly along designated routes; each center is assigned a certain airspace containing many different routes. En route controllers work in teams of up to three members, depending on how heavy traffic is; each team is responsible for a section of the center's airspace. A team, for example, might be responsible for all planes that are between thirty and one hundred miles north of an airport and flying at an altitude between six thousand and eighteen thousand feet.

• **Flight service specialists.** In addition to airport towers and en route centers, air traffic controllers also work in flight service stations operated at more than one hundred locations. These flight service specialists provide pilots with information on the station's particular area, including terrain, preflight and in-flight weather information, suggested routes, and other information important to the safety of a flight. Flight service specialists help pilots in emergency situations and initiate and coordinate searches for missing or overdue aircraft. However, they are not involved in actively managing air traffic.

## U.S. Air Traffic Control

Some air traffic controllers work at the FAA's Air Traffic Control Systems Command Center in Herndon, Virginia, where they oversee the entire air traffic control system. They look for situations that will create bottlenecks or other problems and then respond with a management plan for traffic into and out of the troubled sector. The objective is to keep traffic levels in the trouble spots manageable for the controllers working at en route centers.

The FAA has implemented an automated air traffic control system, called the National Airspace System (NAS) Architecture. The NAS Architecture is a long-term strategic plan that will allow controllers to more efficiently deal with the demands of increased air traffic. It encompasses the replacement of aging equipment and the introduction of new systems, technologies, and procedures to enhance safety and security and support future aviation growth.

The NAS Architecture facilitates continuing discussion of modernization between the FAA and the aviation community.

## NAV CANADA

NAV CANADA is a private sector corporation that owns and operates Canada's civil air navigation service (ANS). It is responsible for coordinating the safe and efficient movement of aircraft in Canadian domestic airspace and international airspace assigned to Canadian control. NAV CANADA provides air traffic control, flight information, weather briefings, aeronautical information, airport advisory services, and electronic aids to navigation.

ANS facilities include seven area control centers and forty-two control towers. The company also operates sixty flight service stations and seven flight information centers. These facilities are supported by a network of more than one thousand ground-based aids to navigation located across the country.

The ANS employs more than five thousand people across Canada in the following capacities: air traffic controllers, flight service specialists, electronic technologists, air traffic operations specialists, and other positions as engineers, pilots, technical support personnel, administrative staff, and management.

Air traffic controllers must be articulate to give pilots directions quickly and clearly. Intelligence and a good memory also are important because controllers constantly receive information that they must immediately grasp, interpret, and remember. Decisiveness also is required because controllers often have to make quick decisions. The ability to concentrate is crucial because controllers must make these decisions in the midst of noise and other distractions.

At airports, new controllers begin by supplying pilots with basic flight data and airport information. They advance to the position of ground controller, then local controller, departure controller, and, finally, arrival controller. At an air route traffic control center, new controllers first deliver printed flight plans to teams, gradually advancing to radar associate controller and then radar controller.

## *Qualifications and Training*

To become an air traffic controller, you must enroll in an FAA-approved education program and pass a preemployment test that measures your ability to learn the controller's duties. The only exceptions are air traffic controllers with prior experience and military veterans. The preemployment test is currently offered only to students in the FAA Air Traffic Collegiate Training Initiative Program or the Minneapolis Community and Technical College, Air Traffic Control Training Program. The test is administered by computer and takes about eight hours to complete. In addition to the preemployment test, applicants must have three years of full-time work experience, have completed a full four years of college, or have a combination of both. Certain kinds of aviation experience may be substituted for these requirements. Candidates must pass a medical exam, undergo drug screening, and obtain a security clearance before they can be hired.

Upon selection, you will attend the FAA Academy in Oklahoma City, Oklahoma, for twelve weeks of training, during which you'll learn the fundamentals of the airway system, FAA regulations, controller equipment, and aircraft performance characteristics, as well as more specialized tasks.

After graduation, you will be classified as "developmental controller" until you complete all requirements to be certified for all of the air traffic control positions within a defined area of a given facility. Generally, it takes new controllers with only initial controller training between two and four years, depending on the facility and the availability of facility staff or contractors to provide on-the-job training, to complete all the certification requirements to become certified professional controllers. Individuals who have had prior controller experience normally take less time to become fully certified. Controllers who fail to complete either the academy or the on-the-job portion of the training usually are dismissed. Controllers must pass a physical examination each year and a job performance examination twice each year. Failure to become certified in any position at a facility within a specified time also may result in dismissal. Controllers are subject to drug screening as a condition of continuing employment.

Controllers can transfer to jobs at different locations or advance to supervisory positions—including management or staff jobs such as air traffic control data systems computer specialist—in air traffic control and in top administrative jobs in the FAA.

To be employed in Air Traffic Services by NAV CANADA, you must be eighteen years of age and a Canadian citizen or landed immigrant. The minimum education requirement is a high school diploma. You must pass a medical exam and secret-level security check before being admitted to the ATS Training Program. The program is conducted at the NAV CANADA Training Institute in Cornwall, Ontario. The education you will receive in the training program is basically the same as that offered by the FAA to American applicants.

Once you've completed all training requirements, you will become a probationary employee with pay and sent for qualification training to a flight information center, flight service station, or control tower. The career path you choose and the needs of NAV CANADA will determine where you may be assigned.

## *Earnings and Benefits*

Air traffic controllers earn relatively high pay and have good benefits. In 2004 median annual earnings were $102,030, with the majority earning between $78,170 and $126,260. In the U.S. federal government, which employs 90 percent of all air traffic controllers, the average salary in 2004 was $106,380.

In 2006, controllers employed by NAV CANADA had average annual earnings of $59,502.

Depending on length of service, air traffic controllers receive thirteen to twenty-six days of paid vacation and thirteen days of paid sick leave each year, in addition to life insurance and health benefits. Controllers also can retire at an earlier age and with fewer years of service than other federal employees. Air traffic controllers are eligible to retire at age fifty with twenty years of service as an active air traffic controller or after twenty-five years of active service at any age. There is a mandatory retirement age of fifty-six for controllers who manage air traffic. However, federal law provides for exemptions to the mandatory age up to age sixty-one for controllers having exceptional skills and experience.

# Federal Regulatory Agencies

It should be noted that many of the positions in the federal agencies concerned with transportation call for specialists in accounting, data processing, engineering, finance, highway traffic, personnel, planning, research, safety, and transportation. In addition, there are the usual office support positions in the clerical areas.

For information about current job openings, visit the official government employment website at www.usajobs.com.

## *Department of Transportation (DOT)*

This department establishes the nation's transportation policy. The top priorities of the DOT are maintaining the safety and security of the traveling public and ensuring that the transportation system contributes to the country's economic growth.

The DOT employs nearly sixty thousand people across the country in the following administrations and bureaus:

- Office of the Secretary of Transportation (OST)
- Federal Aviation Administration (FAA)
- Federal Highway Administration (FHWA)
- Federal Motor Carrier Safety Administration (FMCSA)
- Federal Railroad Administration (FRA)
- Federal Transit Administration (FTA)
- Maritime Administration (MARAD)
- National Highway Traffic Safety Administration (NHTSA)
- Office of the Inspector General (OIG)
- Pipeline and Hazardous Materials Safety Administration (PHMSA)
- Research and Innovative Technology Administration (RITA)
- Saint Lawrence Seaway Development Corporation (SLSDC)
- Surface Transportation Board (STB)

Each administration has its own management and organizational structure. For complete information about DOT bureaus and the career opportunities, visit www.dot.gov. Links to individual administrations are available through the website.

## *Transportation Security Administration (TSA)*

The Transportation Security Administration, formed immediately following the terrorist attacks of September 11, 2001, is a component of the Department of Homeland Security. The TSA is responsible for security of the nation's transportation systems.

Working with state, local, and regional partners, the TSA oversees security for the nation's highways, railroads, buses, mass transit systems, ports, and some 450 airports. The administration employs approximately fifty thousand people from Alaska to Puerto Rico—perhaps the most visible of these workers are the security officers who screen passengers and baggage prior to boarding commercial flights. Visit www.tsa.gov for complete information on the administration.

## *Federal Maritime Commission*

This commission regulates the waterborne foreign and domestic offshore commerce of the country. It ensures that United States' international trade is open to all nations on fair and equitable terms and protects against unauthorized activity in the waterborne commerce of the United States.

For further information, visit www.fmc.gov.

## *Transport Canada*

Transport Canada is the federal department responsible for most of the transportation policies, programs, and goals established by the government to ensure that the national transportation system is safe, efficient, and accessible to all its users. Its mission is to have a transportation system that is safe and secure, efficient, and environmentally responsible.

The department employs approximately forty-seven hundred people at headquarters in Ottawa and in locations across Canada. Those employed at the Ottawa offices work in the following areas:

- Policy overview
- Safety and security
- Programs group
- Corporate services
- Departmental general counsel
- Communications

Transport Canada also has five regional offices serving the following areas: Pacific, Prairie and Northern, Ontario, Quebec, and Atlantic. For information about Transport Canada's services, visit www.tc.gc.ca.

## State, Provincial, and Local Regulatory Agencies

Another layer of agencies regulating intrastate transportation may be found in each of the states and provinces. They have various names, the most usual being the "public utilities commission," although you may find "department of transportation" or even "railroad commission." Since their jurisdictions are limited to operations within the state or province, most of them offer limited career opportunities. You can obtain the name and address of your state agency from your public library or by writing to the secretary of state at your state capital. You may find openings for drivers and mechanics with the highway department. Contact the nearest state or provincial employment security office or the civil service commission for information about current job openings.

In some of the larger municipalities, you may find agencies that regulate taxi and limousine service within the city borders or the operation of the transit system. There may be an agency that provides automobiles and drivers to transport municipal employees on official business. As in the case of the state, the highway department may offer job opportunities for drivers, mechanics, and other job assignments. Consult your telephone book under the listing for your city for the proper name of such agencies, or visit the civil service commission.

## *Job Requirements and Earnings*

To obtain the most current information about job requirements and salaries for federal, state, and provincial positions, it is best to contact the departments and agencies directly.

Information about specific job requirements and salaries is available at www.usajobs.com, the official job posting site of the federal government. To learn more about job opportunities in Canada, visit www.jobs-emplois.gc.ca, the website of the Public Commission of Canada.

For information about state and provincial openings, visit the website of your state or province to learn the requirements and salary structure for jobs that are of interest to you.

# 10

## OTHER OPPORTUNITIES IN TRANSPORTATION

THERE ARE OTHER options for careers in transportation that you might not have thought of. One is working with the professionals who plan all those trips that are taken by car, plane, train, or ship. Another involves the very places where we catch that plane, train, or ship. And a third option is to work with the people who help travelers in need.

## Travel Agents

Travel agencies are by no means as new as might be expected. As early as 1841 an Englishman, Thomas Cook, planned the first guided tours for small parties. In 1852 he publicly advertised Cook's Tours to attract tourists eager to travel abroad. Twenty years later a travel agency opened in the United States, and from that small start a large industry took root and grew to some twenty thousand professional consultants.

Today travel agents not only secure bus, cruise, plane, and train tickets as well as reservations for rental cars and hotel rooms, they also act as travel consultants and travel salespersons. Some even organize their own tours and act as guides or book their clients on tours conducted by other organizations. Four of the largest are AAA (American Automobile Association), American Express, Carlson/Wagonlit Travel, and Thomas Cook & Son.

Constantly changing airfares and schedules, thousands of available vacation packages, and a vast amount of travel information on the Internet can make travel planning frustrating and time consuming. To sort out the many travel options, tourists and businesspeople often turn to travel agents, who assess their needs and help them make the best possible travel arrangements. Also, many major cruise lines, resorts, and specialty travel groups use travel agents to promote travel packages to millions of people every year.

In general, travel agents give advice on destinations and make arrangements for transportation, hotel accommodations, car rentals, tours, and recreation. They also may advise on weather conditions, restaurants, and tourist attractions. For international travel, agents also provide information on customs regulations, required papers (passports, visas, and certificates of vaccination), and currency exchange rates.

Travel agents consult a variety of published and computer-based sources for information on departure and arrival times, fares, and hotel ratings and accommodations. They may personally visit hotels, resorts, and restaurants to evaluate comfort, cleanliness, and quality of food and service so that they can base recommendations on their own travel experiences or those of colleagues or clients.

To establish a clientele, travel agents must promote their services, using telemarketing, direct mail, and the Internet. They make presentations to social and special-interest groups, arrange advertising displays, and suggest company-sponsored trips to business managers. Travel agents no longer receive commissions from domestic airlines, and agents face increasing competition from the Internet for low-cost fares. To find a niche in the market, many agents now specialize in travel to certain regions or for certain groups of people, such as honeymooners, grandparents, or ethnic groups.

## Job Training

The minimum requirement for working as a travel agent is a high school diploma or equivalent. However, since technology and computerization have increased the training needs, you will find more opportunities if you have additional education, such as a postsecondary vocational award. Many vocational schools offer full-time travel agent programs that last several months, as well as evening and weekend programs.

You can also find travel agent courses in public adult education programs and in community and four-year colleges. A few colleges offer bachelor's or master's degrees in travel and tourism. Although few college courses relate directly to travel or tourism, some employers look for a college education to establish a background in fields such as computer science, geography, communication, foreign languages, and world history. Courses in accounting and business management also are important, especially if you plan to manage or start your own travel agency.

The American Society of Travel Agents offers a correspondence course that provides a basic understanding of the travel industry. You will receive on-the-job training once you are hired by an agency. All employers require computer skills if the job will involve the operation of airline and centralized reservation systems.

Continuing education is critical, as the abundance of travel information readily available through the Internet and other sources has resulted in a more informed consumer who wants to deal with an expert when choosing a travel agent. Experienced agents can take advanced self-study or group-study courses from the Travel Institute, leading to the Certified Travel Counselor designation. The Travel Institute also offers marketing and sales skills development programs and destination specialist programs, which provide detailed knowledge of regions such as North America, Western Europe, the Caribbean, and the Pacific Rim. With the trend toward more specialization, these and other destination specialist courses are increasingly important. Visit www.thetravelinstitute.com for information.

Personal travel experience or experience as an airline reservation agent is an asset because knowledge about a city or foreign country often helps influence a client's travel plans. Patience and the ability to gain the confidence of clients also are useful qualities. To be a successful travel agent, you should be well organized, accurate, and meticulous in order to compile information from various sources and plan and organize your clients' travel itineraries. If you plan to specialize in business travel, you must work quickly and efficiently because business travel often must be arranged on short notice.

As the Internet has become an important tool for making travel arrangements, more travel agencies are using websites to provide their services to clients. This trend has increased the importance of computer skills in this occupation. Other desirable qualifications include good writing and interpersonal and sales skills.

As a new employee, you may start as reservation clerk or receptionist in a travel agency. With experience and some formal training, you can take on greater responsibilities and eventually assume travel agent duties. In agencies with many offices, you may advance to office manager or to other managerial positions.

Those who start their own agencies generally have had experience in an established agency. Before they can receive commissions, these agents usually must gain formal approval from suppliers or corporations, such as airlines, ship lines, or rail lines. The Airlines Reporting Corporation and the International Airlines Travel Agency Network, for example, are the approving bodies for airlines. To gain approval, an agency must be financially sound and employ at least one experienced manager or travel agent.

There are no federal licensing requirements for travel agents. In 2004, however, thirteen states required some form of registration or certification of retail sellers of travel services. More information may be obtained by contacting the office of the attorney general or department of commerce in each state.

## Earnings

A travel agent's salary is determined by experience, sales ability, and the size and location of the agency. In 2004 median annual earnings of travel agents were $27,640; the majority earned between $21,600 and $35,070, while the lowest 10 percent earned less than $17,180, and the top 10 percent earned more than $44,090.

Salaried agents usually enjoy standard employer-paid benefits that self-employed agents must provide for themselves. When traveling for personal reasons, agents usually get reduced rates for transportation and accommodations. In addition, they sometimes take "familiarization" trips, at lower cost or no cost to themselves, to learn about various vacation sites. These benefits attract many people to this occupation.

Earnings of travel agents who own their agencies depend mainly on commissions from travel-related bookings and service fees they charge clients. Often it takes time to acquire a sufficient number of clients to have adequate earnings, so it is not unusual for new self-employed agents to have low earnings. Established agents may have lower earnings during economic downturns.

## Employment Outlook

The Internet increasingly allows people to access travel information from their personal computers, enabling them to research and plan their own trips, make their own reservations and travel arrangements, and purchase their own tickets. As a result, demand will decline for travel agents who simply take orders, such as booking tickets for a specified date and time. Also, because domestic airlines no longer pay commissions to travel agencies, reduced revenues have caused some agencies to go out of business.

This change also has led many travel agents to begin charging fees for their services. To justify those fees, customers expect travel agents to provide good service and travel expertise, so opportunities may be better for agents who specialize in specific destinations, luxury travel, or particular types of travelers, such as ethnic groups or groups with a special interest or hobby. Many consumers still prefer to use a professional travel agent to plan a complete trip; to deal with some of the more complex transactions; to ensure reliability; to suggest excursions or destinations that might otherwise be missed; to save time; or, in some cases, to save money.

Several factors should offset the adverse effect of Internet travel arrangement and the loss of revenues from airline bookings. For example, spending on tourism and travel is expected to increase over the next decade. With rising household incomes, smaller families, and an increasing number of older people who are more likely to travel, more people are expected to take vacations—and to do so more frequently—than in the past. Business travel also should rebound from recession and terrorism-related declines as business activity expands. In addition, as U.S. businesses open more foreign operations and businesses increasingly sell their goods and services worldwide, business travel will increase. Luxury and specialty travel should also increase among the growing number of Americans with the available time and money for these more expensive trips.

Another positive factor is the increasing affordability of air travel. Greater competition among airlines, especially from low-cost carriers, has made airfares affordable for more people. In addition, American travel agents now organize more tours for the growing number of foreign visitors. Also, travel agents often are able to offer various travel packages at a substantial discount.

The demand for travel is sensitive to economic downturns and international political crises, when travel plans are likely to be deferred. Therefore, the number of job opportunities for travel agents fluctuates. However, the number of travelers has risen recently, possibly reflecting demand from consumers who delayed travel because of terrorism and safety concerns. Demand for travel remains volatile, though, and trends could change at any time.

## Value of Terminals

No doubt the first transportation terminals served a railroad and consisted of shelters erected at each end of a short railroad line. Terminals as we think of them today are stations that serve as a junction between two or more carriers. During the 1800s, as more railroads were built and met other rail lines where they could exchange passengers and freight, terminals grew in importance and size until most large cities serviced by several roads boasted imposing structures that offered many amenities.

Without a doubt Grand Central Terminal in New York City became the most famous terminal. Its huge concourse marked by the star-studded ceiling above and the famous, round, shiny information booth below; its spacious hallways extending in every direction to connect with office buildings, hotels, and stores; and its countless shops and restaurants have made it a landmark. It has been said that a person could live in a hotel with an underground entrance to Grand Central and obtain everything he or she needed without ever going outdoors.

Today other large sprawling terminals at major airports offer a wide variety of services and stores. You can walk seemingly forever from one end to the other of Chicago's O'Hare Airport terminal, while in other large and newer terminals, connecting airline passengers ride on people movers or monorail trains.

### Today's Terminals

Any weekday at five o'clock visit Seattle's ferry terminal, one of Chicago's commuter railroad terminals, or the mammoth New York Port Authority Bus Terminal. As you watch the thousands of men and women rushing to catch ferries, planes, trains, or buses, you will realize what important places terminals can be. Even the small terminal in Vermont's White River Junction, which serves Greyhound and Vermont Transit buses, can be a hectic place as frantic passengers run up to the single window for tickets or information and the loudspeaker blares "Last call for New York City on platform three!" The difference between this terminal and the one in New York is a matter of size, but the operations and problems are similar.

What is a modern terminal? Simply stated, it is a place from which passengers, freight, and express items depart and arrive. Whatever form of transportation it may serve, a terminal must supply facilities for loading and unloading passengers and freight and, in the case of a passenger terminal, provide waiting rooms, restaurant(s), and comfort facilities, as well as ready access to ground transportation. In addition it should be possible to fuel, clean, provision, and repair the planes, trains, vehicles, or ships. Thus a wide range of workers is needed to provide all the services required.

The organization and management of terminals vary widely. At a large airport each airline may have its own terminal, which is part of the overall complex. At a small airport, the terminal may serve two or three airlines but have a consolidated ticket office with baggage handlers, mechanics, and fleet service workers. These workers are employees of the terminal company. Some bus terminals offer consolidated services with two or more lines using the facilities. In the case of railroads or ferries, where usually only one carrier arrives and departs, one group of employees provides all the necessary services.

Whatever the arrangements, they are of little consequence to you if you are investigating career possibilities at a terminal. However, you should bear in mind that if you are a mechanic, for example, you might find that the terminal management has no such job openings because each of the carriers uses its own employees. On the other hand, were you interested in a reservations or ticketing position, you might learn that the terminal company provides these services to all the carriers, and it is the place to apply. The best way to discover what job openings there are is to visit the terminal's personnel office.

We have already covered the career opportunities available with each of the major forms of transportation. As for terminals, regardless of who owns or manages them, they all must maintain grounds and roads; do maintenance for which carpenters, electricians, plumbers, painters, and other craftspersons are required; and provide security and clerical functions. There is also opportunity for unskilled laborers, typists, accountants, and computer specialists.

In large terminals there is a need for a public relations staff, specialists in personnel, planners, and purchasing agents. The top positions would be those of manager and assistant manager, posts for which several years of experience are required.

Most terminals rent space to concessions: restaurants, newsstands, car rental agencies, gift shops, and, in large city terminals, stores of all kinds. Working in a restaurant or store would provide temporary employment and give you an opportunity to check for other openings in the field you want to enter.

## Travelers Aid

In most large terminals, you will find a desk in or near the waiting room where arriving travelers can easily spot it and its sign: "Travelers Aid Society." These services date back to 1851, when the mayor of St. Louis saw the need to help travelers headed west who were stranded in the city. He paid to set up a service to help those who were penniless, homeless, starving, lost, or in need of a job or counseling.

Today, Travelers Aid International is the association for Travelers Aid programs and agencies in the United States, Canada, and

Puerto Rico. In 2005, Travelers Aid served more than five million people in forty-eight communities and at thirty-six transportation centers (airports, bus, and train stations).

Each person helped by Travelers Aid presents a unique problem: A diabetic person has an unanticipated delay in his journey and realizes he needs medicine. A prepaid phone card from Travelers Aid enables a teenager to contact her parents. A woman who can't speak English turns to Travelers Aid for help in contacting her family. More than twenty-four hundred volunteers provide reassurance as well as the information necessary for travelers to make informed decisions. Travelers Aid assists the elderly, persons with disabilities, and anyone who needs extra help to make his or her connections.

Professional counselors offer assistance to those who become stranded by engaging the client in the process of developing a plan that brings an end to the crisis and ensures a safe return home. Primarily an urban phenomenon, Travelers Aid today serves metropolitan areas that, combined, total 110 million or more in terms of population. It is part of the fabric of social service agencies that respond to the needy. Homeless persons and others who feel disconnected in their own communities reach out to Travelers Aid. Whether through a local network referral process or with specific programs geared to provide shelter and food or training and support, Travelers Aid helps clients make the transition from crisis to independence. Examples include helping victims of domestic violence escape the trauma and get to a safe environment, aiding newly employed workers with local transit tickets, providing transitional housing, and serving as advocates to ensure that those in need get the services they require.

For more information, visit www.travelersaid.org.

# 11

---

# YOUR NEXT STEP

BY NOW YOU have seen that transportation, like other industries, offers both advantages and disadvantages. It might be helpful to list them here.

## Advantages

Since transportation is as essential to the nation as agriculture, it offers greater job security than many other businesses. Unlike some industries that may lay off many employees or close down altogether during economic recessions, a carrier may be forced to retrench somewhat, but not to the extent that many harder-hit firms might.

If you like to travel, you may find a position that will enable you to do so. Even though you hold a desk job in an airline, bus, or rail company, you may enjoy free travel privileges along with other fringe benefits. Best of all, this business has glamour because travel can be stimulating and fun.

## Disadvantages

On the other hand, transportation is a seven-day-a-week, around-the-clock business. This means you may be assigned to work the night shift (4:00 P.M. to midnight) or the graveyard shift (midnight to 8:00 A.M.), to say nothing of Saturdays, Sundays, and holidays. Furthermore, if your job involves working on buses, planes, trains, ships, trucks, or other vehicles that travel long distances, you may be away from home a lot. Because air, marine, and ground transport runs year-round in every kind of weather, you can anticipate encountering all types of weather conditions and occasionally dangerous travel conditions.

## Educational Training

After finishing this book, if you think a career in transportation is for you, learn all you can about that branch of the industry and the jobs that interest you. Find out what education or specialized training is required, so that you can start preparing yourself as soon as possible. Discuss your ideas with other people whose judgment you respect or, preferably, someone in the industry.

To summarize what has been said before, transportation jobs require one of four levels of educational training:

1. A high school diploma for unskilled entry positions, such as cleaners, custodians, food handlers, mailroom clerks, and drivers
2. Technical or vocational school for mechanics, secretaries, bookkeepers, pilots, and seamen
3. Undergraduate degree for many entry positions in supervisory or professional positions

4. Graduate degree principally for professional positions such as engineers, lawyers, librarians, computer specialists, management specialists, public relations practitioners, and the like

You are most likely already quite comfortable with a computer, and you know that computers are used to some degree in nearly all jobs. Needless to say, the more computer knowledge you possess, the better off you will be.

Regardless of the educational requirements of the job you are contemplating, start today to chart your future so that you can make it happen. Lack of money need not discourage you or keep you from pursuing a career that calls for technical or college training. Loans and grants are available to most students, and you might be able to earn a scholarship. Contact your high school counselor or visit the financial aid office of a college for more information.

## Seeking Your Career

When you are ready to start your job search, consider the following suggestions:

- Read one or two books on how to find a job. Ask your school or public librarian for recommendations and check the Suggested Reading section at the end of this book.
- If you are in high school or college, ask the guidance counselor or someone in the college personnel office for job leads and advice.
- Tell everyone you know about your job hunting goal because someone may hear of openings.

- Study the help-wanted advertisements in your local newspapers.
- Visit the offices and websites of transport operators where you hope to find work, and ask if you may file an application.
- Finally, don't become discouraged. Keep up your search every day. Remember that you will find a job if you look hard enough.

## The Future Is Yours

Few industries offer the variety of job opportunities that transportation does. Most important, transportation is a business that places an awesome responsibility on you. For example, a nut that is not properly tightened, an underinflated tire, or a restraining block of wood not removed from a wing joint could be the cause of tragedy. During the years ahead, the lives of many men, women, and children could depend on how carefully and conscientiously you perform your duties. As you can see, this is a career not to be undertaken lightly.

Whatever your decision, we wish you success in your chosen career.

# APPENDIX

# *Transportation Associations, Agencies, and Labor Unions*

Air Line Pilots Association, International
1625 Massachusetts Ave. NW
Washington, DC 20036
www.apla.org

Air Transport Association of America
1301 Pennsylvania Ave. NW, Ste. 1100
Washington, DC 20004-1707
www.air-transport.org

Aircraft Mechanics Fraternal Association
14001 E. Iliff Ave., Ste. 217
Aurora, CO 80014
www.amfanatl.org

Allied Pilots Association
14600 Trinity Blvd., Ste. 500
Fort Worth, TX 76155-2512
www.alliedpilots.org

Amalgamated Transit Union
5025 Wisconsin Ave. NW
Washington, DC 20016
www.atu.org

American Maritime Officers
2 W. Dixie Hwy.
Dania Beach, FL 33004
www.amo-union.org

American Public Transportation Association
1666 K St. NW
Washington, DC 20006
www.apta.com

American Road and Transportation Builders Association
1219 28th St. NW
Washington, DC 20007-3389
www.artba.org

American Society of Travel Agents
1101 King St.
Alexandria, VA 22314
www.travelsense.org

American Train Dispatchers Association
1370 Ontario St., Ste. 140
Cleveland, OH 44113
http://atdd.homestead.com/atddpg1.html

American Trucking Association
2200 Mill Rd.
Alexandria, VA 22314
www.truckline.com

Association of American Railroads
50 F St. NW
Washington, DC 20001
www.aar.org

Association of Flight Attendants–CWA
501 3rd St. NW
Washington, DC 20001
www.afanet.org

Brotherhood of Locomotive Engineers and Trainmen
1370 Ontario St., Mezzanine
Cleveland, OH 44113
www.ble.org

Brotherhood of Maintenance of Way Employees
Division of the International Brotherhood of Teamsters
20300 Civic Center Dr., Ste. 320
Southfield, MI 48076-4169
www.bmwe.org

Brotherhood of Railroad Signalmen
917 Shenandoah Shores Rd.
Front Royal, VA 22630-3418
www.brs.org

Brotherhood of the Railway Carmen
Division of Transportation Communications Union
3 Research Pl.
Rockville, MD 20850
http://members.aol.com/tcucarmen/6760home.htm

Canadian Air Transport Security Authority
99 Bank St., 13th Fl.
Ottawa, ON K1P 6B9
www.catsa-acsta.gc.ca

Canadian Coast Guard
Fisheries and Oceans Canada Communications Branch
200 Kent St., 13th Fl., Station 13228
Ottawa, ON K1A 0E6
www.ccg-gcc.gc.ca

Canadian National Railway
935 de La Gauchetière St. W.
Montreal, QC H3B 2M9
www.cn.ca

Canadian Pacific Railway
Gulf Canada Sq.
401 9th Ave. SW
Calgary, AB T2P 4Z4
www8.cpr.ca

Canadian Urban Transit Association
55 York St., Ste. 1401
Toronto, ON M5J 1R7
www.cutaactu.ca

Federal Aviation Administration
800 Independence Ave. SW
Washington, DC 20591
www.faa.gov

Federal Motor Carrier Safety Administration
400 7th St. SW
Washington, DC 20590
www.fmcsa.dot.gov

International Brotherhood of Teamsters
25 Louisiana Ave. NW
Washington, DC 20001
www.teamsters.org

International Longshoremen's Association
17 Battery Pl., Ste. 930
New York, NY 10004
www.ilaunion.org

International Organization of Masters, Mates, and Pilots
700 Maritime Blvd.
Linthicum Heights, MD 21090-1941
www.bridgedeck.org

International Union of Operating Engineers
1125 17th St. NW
Washington, DC 20036
www.iuoe.org

International Union, United Automobile, Aerospace and
   Agricultural Implement Workers of America (UAW)
Solidarity House
8000 E. Jefferson
Detroit, MI 48214
www.uaw.org

Laborers' International Union of North America
www.liuna.org

Marine Engineers' Beneficial Association
444 N. Capitol St., Ste. 800
Washington, DC 20001
www.d1meba.org

Marine Firemen's Union
240 2nd St.
San Francisco, CA 94105
www.mfoww.org

Maritime Administration
U.S. Department of Transportation
400 7th St. SW, Rm. 7302
Washington, DC 20590
www.marad.dot.gov/acareerafloat

Military Sealift Command
APMC, P.O. Box 120
Camp Pendleton
Virginia Beach, VA 23458-0120
www.sealiftcommand.com

National Association of Air Traffic Specialists
P.O. Box 2550
Landover Hills, MD 20784-0550
www.naats.org

NAV CANADA
P.O. Box 3411, Station D
Ottawa, ON K1P 5L6
www.navcanada.ca

Pacific Coast Marine Firemen, Oilers, Watertenders and Wipers
    Association
240 2nd St.
San Francisco, CA 94105
www.mfoww.org

Professional Aviation Maintenance Association
717 Princess St.
Alexandria, VA 22314
www.pama.org

Professional Truck Driver Institute
2200 Mill Rd.
Alexandria, VA 22314
www.ptdi.org

Railway Association of Canada
99 Bank St., Ste. 1401
Ottawa, ON K1P 6B9
www.railcan.ca

Sailors Union of the Pacific
450 Harrison St.
San Francisco, CA 94105
www.sailors.org

Seafarers International Union
5201 Auth Way
Camp Springs, MD 20746
www.seafarers.org

Transport Canada
330 Sparks St.
Ottawa, ON K1A 0N5
www.tg.gc.ca

Transport Workers Union of America
1700 Broadway, 2nd Fl.
New York, NY 10019
www.twu.org

United Auto Workers
Solidarity House
8000 E. Jefferson Ave.
Detroit, MI 48214
www.uaw.org

United Motorcoach Association
113 S. West St., 4th Fl.
Alexandria, VA 22314
www.uma.org

United Transportation Union
14600 Detroit Ave.
Cleveland, OH 44107-4250
www.utu.org

VIA Rail Canada Inc.
Customer Relations
P.O. Box. 8116, Station A
Montréal QC H3C 3N3
www.viarail.ca

# Suggested Reading

The following books should prove interesting and helpful to anyone who wants further information about transportation careers. You may find additional current information about transportation in magazines and journals—a search of amazon.com or browsing through a large bookstore or library will lead you to useful titles.

Adams, Alice. *A Survival Guide for Truck Drivers: Tips from the Trenches (Medium/Heavy Duty Truck)*. Florence, Ky.: Thomson Delmar Learning, 2002.

———. *Trucking Guide to Border Crossing*. Florence, Ky.: Thomson Delmar Learning, 2004.

———. *Trucking Rules and Regulations: Reference Guide to Transportation*. Florence, Ky.: Thomson Delmar Learning, 2004.

Belman, Dale, and Chelsea White III, eds. *Trucking in the Age of Information*. Aldeshot, Hampshire, U.K.: Ashgate Publishing, 2005.

Berger, Michael L. *The Automobile in American History and Culture: A Reference Guide.* Westport, Conn.: Greenwood Press, 2001.

Blow, Christopher. *Transport Terminals and Modal Interchanges.* Burlington, Mass.: Architectural Press, 2005.

Brenlove, Milovan S. *The Air Traffic System: A Commonsense Guide,* 2nd ed. Ames: Iowa State University Press, 2003.

Byrnes, Mike, et al. *Bumper to Bumper: The Complete Guide to Tractor-Trailer Operations,* 4th ed. Corpus Christi, Tex.: Mike Byrnes and Associates, 2003.

Chowdhury, Mashrur A., and Adel W. Sadek. *Fundamentals of Intelligent Transportation Systems Planning.* Artech House, 2003.

Colbert, Judy, and Dee Minic. *Career Opportunities in the Travel Industry.* New York: Facts on File, 2004.

Cook, Andrew. *To Be an Airline Pilot.* Ramsbury, U.K.: Crowood Press, 2007.

Cornish, Geoff. *Battlefield Support: Military Hardware in Action.* Minneapolis: Lerner Publications, 2003.

Crimson, Fred W. *U.S. Military Wheeled Vehicles,* 3rd ed. Minneapolis: Victory Publishing, 2001.

Delius, Peter, and Jacek Slaski. *Airline Design.* Dusseldorf: teNeues Publishing Group, 2005.

Dixon, Michael. *Motormen and Yachting, The Waterfront Heritage of the Automobile Industry.* Grosse Pointe, Mich.: Mervue Publications, 2005.

Dodd, Monroe. *A Splendid Ride: The Streetcars of Kansas City, 1870–1957.* Kansas City, Mo.: Kansas City Star Books, 2002.

Doganis, Regas. *The Airline Business.* New York: Routledge, 2005.

Doyle, David. *Standard Catalog of U.S. Military Vehicles.* Iola, Wis.: Krause Publications, 2003.

Gifford, Jonathan L. *Flexible Urban Transportation*. Kidlington, Oxford, U.K.: Elsevier Science Ltd., 2003.

Goulias, Konstadinos. *Transportation Systems Planning: Methods and Applications*. Boca Raton, Fla.: CRC, 2002.

Grava, Sigurd. *Urban Transportation Systems*. New York: McGraw-Hill, 2002.

Guo, Boyun, et al. *Offshore Pipelines*. Burlington, Mass.: Gulf Professional Publishing, 2005.

Hanson, Susan, and Genevieve Giuliano, eds. *The Geography of Urban Transportation*, 3rd ed. New York: Guilford Press, 2004.

Herbert, Brian. *The Forgotten Heroes: The Heroic Story of the United States Merchant Marine*. New York: Forge Books, 2004.

Jasinski, Irv. *Airline Pilot Interviews: How You Can Succeed in Getting Hired*. Escondido, Calif.: Career Advancement Publications, 2002.

Lewis, Jerre G. *How to Start and Manage an Independent Trucking Business: A Practical Way to Start Your Business*. Interlochen, Mich.: Lewis and Renn Associates, 2004.

Lutz, Jeanne. *Changing Course: One Woman's True Life Adventures as a Merchant Marine*. Far Hills, N.J.: New Horizon Press, 2003.

Mancini, Marc. *Cruising: A Guide to the Cruise Line Industry*, 2nd ed. Clifton Park, N.Y.: Delmar Learning, 2004.

Mattfield, Dirk C. *The Management of Transshipment Terminals*. New York: Springer, 2006.

Maxton, Graeme P., and John Wormald. *Time for a Model Change: Re-Engineering the Global Automotive Industry*. Cambridge: Cambridge University Press, 2004.

McConville, J. *International Maritime Transport*. New York: Routledge, 2005.

McCoy, Mickey. *Airline Wings as a Career*. Victoria, B.C.: Trafford Publishing, 2006.

Milne, Robert, and Marguerite Backhausen. *Opportunities in Travel Careers*, 2nd ed. New York: McGraw-Hill, 2003.

Mom, Gijs. *The Electric Vehicle: Technology and Expectations in the Automobile Age*. Baltimore: Johns Hopkins University Press, 2004.

Monaghan, Kelly. *Home-Based Travel Agent*, 5th ed. Branford, Conn.: The Intrepid Traveler, 2006.

———. *The Travel Agent's Complete Desk Reference*, 4th ed. Branford, Conn.: The Intrepid Traveler, 2006.

National Learning Corp., (ed.). *Senior Highway Transportation Specialist*. New York: National Learning Corp., 2005.

Nolan, Michael S. *Fundamentals of Air Traffic Control*, 4th ed. Belmont, Calif.: Brooks Cole, 2003.

Parker, Philip M. *The 2007–2012 World Outlook for Automobile Manufacturing*. San Diego: ICON Group International, 2006.

Payne, Christopher. *New York's Forgotten Substations: The Power Behind the Subway*. Princeton, N.J.: Princeton Architectural Press, 2002.

Post, Robert C. *Urban Mass Transit: The Life Story of a Technology*. Westport, Conn.: Greenwood Press, 2006.

Rawlins, Michael R. *The Last American Sailors: A Wild Ride in the Modern Merchant Marine*. Lincoln, Neb.: iUniverse, 2003.

Rhodes, Michael. *North American Railyards*. St. Paul, Minn.: MBI Publishing, 2003.

Shaw, Stephen. *Airline Marketing and Management*, 5th ed. Burlington, Vt.: Ashgate Publishing, 2005.

Shively, Bob, and John Ferrare. *Understanding Today's Natural Gas Business.* Laporte, Colo.: Enerdynamics, 2005.

Smith, Patrick. *Ask the Pilot.* New York: Riverhead Books, 2004.

Solomon, Brian. *Railway Maintenance Equipment: The Men and Machines That Keep the Railroads Running.* St. Paul, Minn.: MBI Publishing, 2001.

————. *Working on the Railroad.* Osceola, Wis.: Voyageur Press, 2006.

Stewart, Paul, and Elsie Charron, eds. *Work and Employment Relations in the Automobile Industry.* New York: Palgrave MacMillan, 2004.

Sussman, Joseph S. *Perspectives on Intelligent Transportation Systems.* New York: Springer, 2006.

U.S. Department of Defense. *21st Century Complete Guide to U.S. Navy Military Sealift Command.* Progressive Management, 2003.

# About the Author

Adrian A. Paradis was born in Brooklyn, New York, and graduated from Dartmouth College and Columbia University's School of Library Service. As a writer, businessman, vocational specialist, and researcher, he has published widely, with more than forty titles to his credit. He has covered subjects that range from banking to biographies, from public relations to religion, from vocational guidance to reference works, and from law to economics.

Paradis spent more than twenty years as an officer of a major national corporation handling corporate matters, economic analysis, stockholder relations, corporate philanthropic contributions, security, and general administrative responsibilities. He lives in Sugar Hill, New Hampshire, where he serves as editor of Phoenix Publishing, a small firm that specializes in regional trade books and New England town histories.

The author wishes to thank Josephine Scanlon for her assistance in preparing this edition.